Unforgettable

things to do

before you die

Unforgettable

things to do

before you die

Steve Watkins and Clare Jones

FIREFLY BOOKS

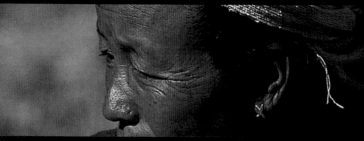

CONTENTS

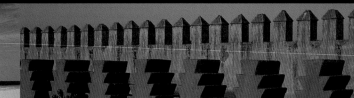

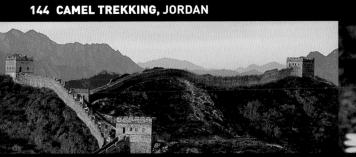

Although there are many great travel experiences, something beyond the ordinary is needed to make a trip truly unforgettable. That extra dose of long-term, memory-clinging satisfaction can come courtesy of anything – from an encounter with nature at its most sublime or a journey through a landscape beyond the imagination, to discovering a whole new way of seeing things. All it really comes down to is being aware of the opportunities and just how accessible they are.

Within 24 hours you can transport yourself from staring out of an office window to riding on horseback across a Mongolian plain. You could be trying to beat the rush hour on a Friday evening and enjoying the bustle of shopping in a Moroccan souk by Saturday afternoon. The desire to escape normal life and do something different is in all of us and, according to travel trends, we are increasingly doing just that. More people than ever before are foregoing standard beach holidays for the chance of an experience that engages the mind, body and spirit – perhaps all three.

Despite extensive media coverage of troubles around the world, the planet is still an awe-inspiring and beautiful place; and many spots, more than can possibly be imagined, remain special and peaceful. Whether it is a magical experience, shared with 15,000 others, watching an opera in a Roman amphitheatre in Verona, Italy, or being alone in one of the earth's wild places – a sea of mountainous dunes on Namibia's Skeleton Coast, for example – the effect is the same. Your spirits soar.

The destinations we chose for our 40 unforgettable things to do are amazing in themselves, but many of our most magical memories are of the smallest of details, the briefest of moments. Seeing a grizzly bear snuffling for ground squirrels in autumn twilight in the Canadian Rockies; enjoying the excitement of husky dogs eager to dash into fresh Swedish snow; watching an isolated young wildebeest unknowingly turn away from an imminent dawn encounter with a hyena on the Serengeti plain. These are the fleeting images, the dramatic and sublime moments that make exploring the planet special. It was impossible to capture all of them on film, though we tried, and this project, more than most, made us realize that an important part of any travel experience is knowing when to put the camera aside and simply observe.

We hope you enjoy reading about our unforgettable experiences, but it is unlikely they will match your own. They are simply here to stir memories of things you may have already done or as an inspiration for future travel – and to provide an insight into the diversity and wonder of our unique planet and the adventures it offers.

The map on pages 252–3 shows the locations of all the places featured in this book. Our choices were based on a number of criteria. Primarily, all the trips can be done within two weeks, many within one, and most can be undertaken with varying levels of independence. There is no need to pack in your job to sample any of them. Some of the more obvious omissions, like the Great Barrier Reef in Australia and America's Grand Canyon, can be found in the first book in this series: *Unforgettable Places to See Before You Die* by Steve Davey.

Where possible, we tried to do the trips with an extra dose of style to ensure they were truly unforgettable. A safari in the Serengeti is wonderful however you choose to travel; but having a private vehicle for two, a spacious tented camp with gourmet meals and an expert, personal guide who spots animals in his sleep takes the experience way beyond the ordinary. With some research, there are often ways to do similar trips on smaller budgets – though we found that the 'luxury' extras were invariably worth paying for! We also wanted to have a good geographical spread around the globe, and to feature places that are visually different.

Our research was undertaken over an exciting and challenging year during which we travelled to five continents, covering more than 280,000 km, and took photographs in desert heat, rainforest humidity and freezing cold. We also had to find time to organize our travels and were helped by a host of people, companies and organizations, who are listed on pages 254–5. We chose to take trips that are on offer to everyone, so what you read and see is what you will probably get, although some experiences may require an early alarm call or skipping dinner!

Whether you only ever do one of the unforgettable things in this book, have already had many memorable travel experiences, or simply enjoy being inspired without venturing far from your armchair, you are part of the community of travellers – people who dare to let their imaginations run free in their desire to explore the world around them.

Steve Watkins and Clare Jones, 2005

Frozen in Jämtland's winter wonderland, the fir forests, ice lakes and gentle mountains around Klocka make it a little-known nirvana for dog-sledding. With the chilly temperatures and vigorous activity that come as standard with this activity, it is only fair to treat your body to a traditional Swedish sauna (icy plunge pool optional) and some high-end Swedish design at the end of the day. Unheralded Klocka just happens to have it all.

Bordering Norway in the Sylarna mountain area, the tiny, old farming village of Klocka is set on the shore of enchanting Lake Ånnsjön. Reindeer roam the water's edges and birds of prey circle overhead.

Husky dogs

The wildness is tempered only by Klocka Fjällgård, an old farmhouse converted by the renowned Swedish furniture designer Nirvan Richter into a chilled-out boutique hotel with that all-important sauna.

Before the calm though, comes the husky storm. Be warned: the mere sniff of a sled outing (just your arrival at the kennels will be enough) sends these intelligent and characterful dogs into howling, bouncing, bog-eyed raptures. All the chaos and noise of harnessing them to the sled line, from the lead dogs to the rear 'wheel' dogs, converts to raw power once the snow anchor is released. As Klocka musher Kari-Mette remarked: 'You don't have to teach them to pull, you have to teach them to stop!'

It is impossible not to be won over by the huskies' strength, enthusiasm and good nature. Hurtling along narrow, forest trails

Heading into the low lying Vallrun hills

Huskies can pull sleds for over 50 km a day

there is a beautiful moment of transition from the initial, unbridled power surge, as the dogs, their deep-seated pack-hunting skills driving them on, all fall into the same loping rhythm and the rails of the sled swish effortlessly through the deep snow.

As you wind up through patchy forest into the Vallrun hills north-east of Klocka the winter sun, which never rises very high above the horizon, casts long shadows of the bounding dogs and the sled. Its gentle warmth is welcome as the temperatures here are regularly well below freezing. For dog-sledding, put on all your warmest clothes, then add more. You may move with all the grace of an injured hippo-potamus, but the cold can bite its way through anything less.

The wild, mountain lake of Södra Gråsjön is the only truly flat and open part of the journey, and as you slide across it your feeling of freedom and communing with nature reaches a high, with your new-found sled-handling skills encouraging you to attempt sweeping turns and higher speeds. Barking out orders to the huskies to turn left and right, you can't help but notice the dogs' slightly confused

Dawn over a fog-filled Lake Ånnsjön at Klocka Fjällgård

Deep red sunrise at Klocka Fjällgård

glances over their shoulders. They are very willing and obedient, but they can also spot a novice musher at a hundred metres. Reality returns, and the dogs seemingly make their own way up a steep incline to a beautiful hillside look-out and a food stop at Gråsjölien.

This is no Alaska with oversized scenery, but the whole beauty of dog-sledding is that it gels perfectly with the beautifully sculptured landscape. The mountains, like distant Sylarna and Bunnerfjällen, are high enough, but their slopes seem to melt rather than plunge into the lightly fir-forested valley. The dogs love running here, and even before the last crumbs of a fire-toasted sandwich have been devoured, their tails start to wag and their powerful legs start to stretch. As they haul at their harnesses, eager to charge home in the fading afternoon light, it seems the pack is at last finely tuned into the thoughts of just about any novice musher. For surely, only the desire to relax in a sauna can inspire such breakneck speed on the return journey.

Dawn over Lake Ånnsjön

ⓘ ⋯⋯⋯⋯⋯⋯⋯⋯⋯⋯⋯⋯⋯⋯⋯⋯⋯⋯⋯⋯⋯⋯⋯

Klocka's dog-sledding season runs from about mid-December to late April, depending on the snow conditions, with February onwards tending to be the best time as it is slightly warmer. The nearest airport to Klocka is at Östersund, 125 km away, which is served several times daily by Scandinavian Airlines (SAS) from Stockholm. The wonderful boutique hotel, Klocka Fjällgård, organizes snowmobiling and other activities as well as dog-sledding, and arranges transfers to and from Östersund airport.

Aboriginal dreaming
Kakadu, Australia

Dubbed 'God's Own Country', the remote Northern Territory is the wildest ingredient in Australia's smorgasbord of wilderness offerings, and home to the country's largest and most fascinating national park: Kakadu. Roughly the same size as Switzerland, and a UNESCO World Heritage Area, Kakadu National Park is an intoxicating mix of pristine wetlands, wild creatures and ancient Aboriginal mythology. If you are thinking of visiting Australia, a four-wheel-drive safari in magnificent Kakadu should be high on your list of things to do.

Cathedral termite mounds tower over Kakadu's bushland

Four-wheel-drive is essential to explore Kakadu

Lying a couple of hundred kilometres south-east of the state capital, Darwin, and easily reached by the Stuart Highway, Kakadu is based around the South Alligator river system. A visit to the park, with its 1600-plus plant species, 300 bird species, 5000 known Aboriginal rock-art sites and more than its fair share of crocodiles, is akin to stepping back in time to the days following the extinction of the dinosaurs. It may be easy to get to, but once there the park induces immediate feelings of dislocation from our technology-filled world.

Nourlangie Rock from Gunwardewarde Lookout

A hardy cycad plant

Kakadu's infrastructure is superb and many places are accessible from the main park road, including the not-to-be-missed Aboriginal rock-art extravaganza at Nourlangie Rock, an outlier of the Arnhem Land escarpment. The 20,000-year-old art gallery is in a series of caves and shallow rock-shelters around this massive, flat-topped sandstone outcrop. For a better appreciation of the rock's dramatic location, walk the marked trail in reverse and see it first from Gunwardewarde Lookout.

Infused with stories about the main protagonists from the Aboriginal dreamtime (by which native Australians mean the time of creation), Nourlangie Rock boasts an array of well-preserved artworks, ranging in age from the beginning of human history to more modern repainting in the 1970s. Prime importance is given to the Anbangbang Gallery, tucked into the base of an overhanging boulder, where a creation ancestor, Namondjok, is depicted alongside a bizarre, white skeletal figure known as Namarrgon, the Lightning Man.

Impressive as the easily accessed sites are, finding Kakadu's real gems requires a four-wheel-drive vehicle and an experienced guide to tackle the myriad off-road tracks. Maguk, or Barramundi Gorge, is located down a long, narrow, sandy track where emus, kangaroos and staccato-songed kookaburra birds are just some of the exotic fauna to be seen. With the humid, hot conditions and lengthy hike to reach Maguk, its idyllic pools would be tempting even if there were crocodiles in them!

Another gem, unmarked on any map and rarely mentioned in guidebooks, is Graveside Gorge, a paradisiacal, two-tiered, waterfall-fed swimming hole. Surrounded by red, rock walls, it is accessed via a beautiful trail lined with 'cathedral' termite mounds that look like towering fins, and hardy cycads. These plants, which have survived

Nabulwinjbulwinj, a dangerous spirit

Little-known Graveside Gorge is perfect for swimming – but watch out for crocodiles!

two periods of mass extinction on the planet, have tough, palm-like leaves and can live for 2500 years.

When you have seen Kakadu from the land, a perfect way to round off the adventure is to board a boat for a trip on Yellow Waters, a pristine wetland that forms part of the South Alligator River's flood plain. On grassy areas sea eagles, jabirus and magpie geese create a birdwatcher's dreamland, while among the mangrove swamps awesome saltwater crocodiles lurk in the shadows. These scaly-backed predators are remnants of the dinosaur era and, no matter how big your boat is, your heart will palpitate when they slide towards you beneath the murky water. One way or another, Kakadu is sure to leave you wide-eyed and more in touch with your wilder side.

ⓘ ⋯⋯⋯⋯⋯⋯⋯⋯⋯⋯⋯⋯⋯⋯⋯⋯⋯⋯⋯⋯⋯⋯⋯⋯⋯⋯⋯⋯⋯⋯⋯⋯

Darwin is served by several international airlines, including Qantas Airlines and Malaysian Airlines. Qantas and Virgin Blue operate domestic flights in Australia. For more information, check out the Australian Tourism Commission's excellent website (www.australia.com). There are a few hotels around Kakadu, but for a more authentic experience choose an operator, such as Darwin-based Odyssey Safaris, which runs comfortable tented camps in the park. On any hike in Kakadu, the amount of water and sun protection you will need must not be underestimated, as it gets very hot. While crocodile attacks are rare, any warnings, verbal or signed, about swimming should be treated seriously. If in doubt, you should seek the advice of a local park ranger.

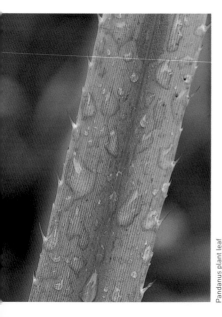

Pandanus plant leaf

Pandanus fruit

Monitor lizard

Hiking towards Maguk Gorge

Crossing the divide
Istanbul, Turkey

Galata Bridge crosses the Golden Horn to Suleymaniye Mosque

The maze-like Grand Bazaar

No place meshes the cultures, history and religions of East and West like Istanbul, Turkey's minaret-spiked cultural capital. From the overwhelming aromatic and spicy shopping overload of the Grand Bazaar and the glorious mosques around Sultanahmet to the chic modern stores of Beyoglu, this intense fusion of Europe and Asia is guaranteed to astonish and bewilder. Yet crossing the divide can readily fit into a long weekend.

First Byzantium, then Constantinople, and now Istanbul, the city straddles the Bosporus strait and its Golden Horn inlet off the Sea of Marmara. Thanks to this geographic location, with Europe on the west side and Asia on the east side of the Bosporus, it has been the focus of

great civilizations across the ages. The Persians, Byzantines, Romans and Ottomans all fought over, occupied and traded through the city. Of all its rulers and emperors, the greatest impact was made by the Ottoman sultan justifiably named Suleiman the Magnificent, who reigned for 46 years from 1520.

It was Suleiman who ordered the building of some of Istanbul's grandest structures, including the sprawling Topkapi Palace, an

Worshippers preparing to prey at Suleymaniye Mosque

inspiring starting point for exploring the city. Entered through the imposing Imperial Gate alongside Hagia Sophia, the palace flows down a hill overlooking the Bosporus and the Sea of Marmara. You won't regret going all the way to Seraglio Point at the end of the fourth court for the best view of these; and the café, Mecidiye Pavilion, has a view to queue for. Other highlights are the tiled underground rooms of the Harem, where the sultan's wives and concubines lived, and the Imperial Treasury. And don't ignore a series of inscribed stone tablets spaced around the first court's inner wall.

From Topkapi the ornate gardens of Sultanahmet Square lead to the striking Sultanahmet Mosque with its soaring minarets and sensuous domes. Slipping off your shoes and entering the dimly lit inner sanctum brings immediate calm. Most surfaces are covered with blue tiles, hence it is also known as the Blue Mosque. It is

Hagia Sophia museum

Topkapi Palace

27

Strolling around Topkapi Palace

Mosaic at Topkapi Palace

still a place of worship, so be patient and observe the posted rules at prayer times.

Save the area's best for last and head across the square to the heavily tiled, Byzantine masterpiece Hagia Sophia (Greek for 'holy wisdom'). This building, with its red-washed walls, was originally a church, then a mosque and is now a museum. Rapidly constructed between 532 and 537 as Constantinople's new cathedral, by the Byzantine emperor Justinian, it boasts a vast dome, once the world's largest. Try to get there early to avoid the midday crowds.

From Hagia Sophia head west to the organized chaos of the Grand Bazaar, Istanbul's exotic precursor to modern shopping malls. At times it can seem as though everyone in the city is selling something, from pots and pans and neon cigarette lighters to elaborately woven kilims. It is the Grand Bazaar, though, with its confusing web of vaulted arcades, that epitomizes the city's rich trading history.

Past the university is the Suleymaniye Mosque, an Ottoman gem built by the legendary architect Mimar Sinan in 1557. With over two hundred windows, the interior space is one of the most enchanting in Istanbul's impressive collection of mosques.

The Galata Bridge is home to a lively street market and legions of fishermen. At weekends barely a space can be found along its upper tier as the men of the city attempt to clear the Golden Horn of its fish stocks. On the lower tier there is a host of seafood restaurants, bars and cafés. It is a surprisingly peaceful place to take a breather and watch the omnipresent ferries ply their trade from shore to shore.

Across the bridge and dominating the Beyoglu skyline, the 14th-century Galata Tower is a perfect place to end your trip to Istanbul. A series of steps and a lift take you to the top to enjoy the compelling view of the sun setting over the minarets, and absorb the chaos and sensory overload that is Istanbul. You won't leave unaffected.

Fourth Court at Topkapi Palace

ⓘ ··

Istanbul can be visited year round, although it gets hot in the summer months. The main mosques and sites are quieter early in the day. Most are accessible on foot, although it is rather hilly. Many airlines, including Turkish Airlines, offer several flights a day to Istanbul, where there is accommodation to suit every taste and budget.

Towering minarets spike Istanbul's skyline

Kayaking through mangrove swamps at Placencia Caye

Spa room with a view at Chaa Creek

From the Mayan ruins and deep rainforest of the mountainous interior around Chaa Creek to the tranquil beauty of the Caribbean coastline, the peaceful Central American country of Belize is a delicious mix of cultures and ripe for exploring, whether on foot, by kayak or with a snorkel.

Bordered by Guatemala and Mexico, Belize shares those countries' rich Mayan heritage with outstanding sites like Xunantunich, Caracol and Lubaantun. At its heart are huge wilderness parks, such as the Cockscomb Basin Wildlife Sanctuary where jaguars roam, that rival those of Costa Rica. And then there is that coast. Speckled with numerous cayes (low-lying sandy islands), it boasts the longest barrier reef in the western hemisphere, and the lifestyle there has definitely caught a dose of the chilled-out, laid-back culture of the Caribbean. Quite simply, there is no other country quite like Belize.

El Castillo at Xunantunich

Starting high, Chaa Creek, a beautiful wilderness spa resort set among dense rainforest, sits above the Macal River at the north-western corner of the vast Mountain Pine Ridge Forest Reserve. Its extensive network of hiking trails will keep you exploring for hours as you pass giant palm fronds and a plethora of exotic plants, including red ginger with its lipstick-red flower and bright green foliage, and Belize's national flower, the delicate and enchanting black orchid. As with many rainforests, wildlife is not easy to track down, but the iridescent blue morpho butterfly, with its lazy wingbeat and electric-blue wings, is hard to miss.

The Macal is a tributary of the Mopán River and forms the southern boundary of the forest reserve. It eventually joins the Mopán at San Ignacio, and canoeing or kayaking to this junction makes for an excellent afternoon expedition. The current is usually gentle enough to allow even inexperienced paddlers to tackle the task. The river is home to a plethora of animals and birdlife, such as river otters, kingfishers and egrets.

Stucco masks on El Castillo at Xunantunich

Dawn at Turtle Inn's beach bar

Just a short drive from Chaa Creek are the impressive Mayan ruins of Xunantunich (Stone Lady), accessed from San José Succotz village via a hand-powered ferry across the Mopán. It was built during the Late Classic period, in about AD 650–700, and very little is known about who ruled here – but it was a major ceremonial centre until it was struck by a massive earthquake in about 900. Without doubt, the star attraction is El Castillo at the south side of the main plaza. This 40-metre-high pyramid pierces the skyline and is fronted by a wide, stone stairway. It is some climb to the top, but the views over the surrounding forest and into Guatemala are well worth a little puffing. On the east and west flanks are impressive stucco mask reliefs.

From the highlands, a wondrous road trip down the verdant Hummingbird Highway takes you past the Blue Hole National Park, famed for its crystal-clear sinkhole, and the Cockscomb Basin Wildlife Sanctuary. After travelling further south, along the Southern Highway, you come to the blissful, beach-lined, noodle-thin Placencia peninsula where the totally relaxed Garifuna culture holds sway. On one side is the blue of the Caribbean while on the other are the dark waters of a large lagoon.

In between, just north of the town of Placencia, is Turtle Inn. Owned by film producer Francis Ford Coppola of *Apocalypse Now* fame, it is a piece of Balinese-inspired heaven with the Caribbean lapping at its door. There is no better place to watch the sunrise over the distant cayes and the sunset over the lagoon. While you can choose to do nothing, the sea kayaks the hotel provides beg you to explore a little, and a gentle paddle is enough to reach Placencia Caye, where pelicans dive-bomb around you and mangrove swamps make for slightly eerie side trips. For snorkellers, a boat ride out to the idyllic white sands and turquoise waters of Laughing Bird Caye is totally unforgettable. But with cocktails and a glorious sunset awaiting you at the Turtle Inn beach bar it may be hard to linger too long.

Wings of a blue morpho butterfly

(i) ....

Belize is politically very stable, and is unlike its Central American neighbours in many respects: English, rather than Spanish, is very widely spoken and on the whole the country feels more Caribbean island than Latin. The road infrastructure is improving, but there are only three main roads. Chaa Creek has a range of accommodation in beautiful thatched cabanas and villas. It has a hill-top spa, and use of canoes is included. Both Chaa Creek and Turtle Inn can be booked via Abercrombie & Kent. Several airlines, including British Airways, fly to Belize City.

Turtle Inn at dawn

Vineyards at Château Phelon Segur

Cultural homeland of French wine and producer of some of the world's most revered brands, such as Château Mouton Rothschild and Château Margaux, there is no finer place than Bordeaux to sample the grand complexities of wine-making. Although there are many ways to tour the region and its wineries, the most memorable is to immerse yourself in decadent living at an elegant château and taste vintages under the guidance of a wine expert.

Elegantly set alongside the Garonne and Dordogne rivers, which feed into the Gironde estuary, Bordeaux, with its endless massed ranks of vines, owes its viniculture reputation to the subtle differences in the region's soils and the aspects and altitudes of its terrain. Broadly known as *terroir*, these features are passionately discussed and debated. With a 2000-year history of wine production, the people in this part of south-west France know how one plot of gravel, sand and clay is unlike any other. It is these differences, combined with the near-magical alchemy applied by the head wine-makers at the châteaux, that translate into the array of excellent red, white and dessert wines produced in the region.

Châteaux and wine-tasting

Bordeaux, France

A colonnade of trees leads up to the gates of Château Margaux

Château Pichon-Longueville Baron in Pauillac district

Of Bordeaux's 57 different appellations, or wine districts, perhaps the best known are Saint-Emilion and Médoc, and, of course, Margaux, where the classically elegant château itself is a must-see for both its colonnaded façade and its world-renowned red wines. However, with over 7000 châteaux producing wine in the region, don't ignore the lesser-known ones. Saint-Julien-Beychevelle on the west bank of the Gironde estuary hosts the lovely Château Léoville-Barton, while in the Pomerol district, on the east side, Château Gazin is well worth a visit. Travelling from east to west across the estuary is best done via a gentle ferry ride from Blaye. Along the water's edge, scores of traditional wooden fishing huts are adorned with unique circular nets hanging from long booms.

Although great white wines are made in Bordeaux, the region is particularly renowned for its reds. Cabernet Sauvignon and Merlot are the most widely grown grapes for these, the former for its vigour and tannin and the latter for its softness. Since 1855 wines produced in the Médoc have been classified, to indicate their quality, with Grand Cru the premier choice followed by Cru Bourgeois and Cru Artisan. Very good vintages, like 1961, can go for thousands of pounds a bottle while lesser years can be snapped up for a fraction of this. In towns like Saint-Emilion, a charming twist of cobbled streets, a plethora of wine merchants offer bottles and cases at competitive prices.

Wine-tasting tours can be a little perplexing to the uninitiated, so the guidance of an expert is highly recommended. However, appreciating a wine is more art than science. Although it helps to grasp the importance of its colour, nose and palate, personal opinion counts for much – and style and flair count for everything – when you go about tasting it. Tilt the glass to see through the wine's colour, swirl it around to release the aromas, and then sip and slurp to your heart's content.

Vineyards at dawn near Château Pichon-Longueville Baron

Dinner at Château Léoville-Barton

When the day's sampling is done there is no better way to spend an evening than dining and sleeping in a château like the magnificent Château Pichon-Longueville Baron, which overlooks the Gironde estuary in the Pauillac district. With its elegant, twin-turreted façade fronting on to a mirroring pond it is a majestic sight both during the day and when it's floodlit at night. Several other private châteaux in the region open their doors to select tour operators, while others, such as the nearby Château Cordeillan-Bages, operate as public hotels.

Château Pichon-Longueville Baron floodlit at dusk

A gourmet dinner provides a good opportunity to savour your newly found knowledge, and to try a dessert wine like the wonderfully smooth and sweet Sauterne. Whatever the label or vintage, you can be assured that each drop reflects the unique characteristics of the Bordeaux region and its wine-passionate people.

Wine cellar tours are a must-do

ⓘ ....

Not all châteaux offer accommodation or tours of their wine-making facilities, so it is always worth checking this (and opening times) beforehand. The UK-based tour company Arblaster & Clarke operates tours, led by distinguished wine experts, that include staying at private châteaux like Château Pichon-Longueville Baron. The international airport at Bordeaux is a short drive from the wine-growing areas.

River-running

Zambezi River, Zambia

Tackling powerful grade four and five rapids are the highlight of any descent

Whether it involves getting drenched by one of the seven natural wonders of the world or rafting the planet's most awesome rapids, a journey on the mighty Zambezi River is a guaranteed thrill.

Rising from a small spring in north-western Zambia, the Zambezi, Africa's fourth-largest river, travels a massive 2700 km and traverses six countries on its way to the Indian Ocean. En route this majestic body of water weaves an unmistakable path, and has carved out the spectacular Victoria Falls where, on the border between Zambia and Zimbabwe, the 2-km-wide river plunges more than 100 metres into the steep-sided and ever-deepening Batoka Gorge, a white-water-rafting paradise.

Water explodes over the bow

The tranquillity of the upstream river, home to giraffes, elephants, hippos, crocodiles and innumerable forms of birdlife, is dramatically shattered as the Zambezi approaches the plunging drop of the falls. At peak flood a staggering 550,000 cubic metres of water thunder over the edge every minute, creating serious white-water rapids below.

For the best views of the falls from the Zambian side follow the network of paths to the none too encouragingly named Knife Edge Bridge, where a hair-raising traverse through swirling clouds of spray takes you on to a downstream island in the river with views of the gaping abyss below. As the falls plunge downwards and ricochet off the rocks in the gorge, spray can spiral upwards as high as 500 metres. This remarkable plume of water can be seen up to 70 km away, earning the Victoria Falls their local name: Mosi-oa-tunya (the smoke that thunders).

Safety kayakers follow every raft

The falls are incredible enough in themselves, but the real adventure lies downstream. If pitting your wits against roller-coaster waves, big drops and swirling eddies grabs you, you will find that white-water rafting on the Zambezi is in a class of its own. Depending on the time of year, you may even find yourself bobbing about at the base of the falls in your inflatable raft, with just a paddle for support, before you launch into a descent.

The 25 raftable rapids come one after the other and form the most daunting commercially-run white water anywhere in the world. They are classified as grade five by the British Canoe Union – the official definition is 'extremely difficult, with long and violent rapids, steep gradients, big drops and pressure areas'. If this doesn't get your adrenalin flowing, the names of some of the rapids just might. With titles like 'The Terminator', 'Oblivion' and 'Stairway to Heaven' they give

Flying over Victoria Falls in a microlight provides a sensational view

Rafting on the Zambezi River takes place in the Batoka Gorge

a pretty clear indication that this is a river not to be messed with. A raft can be overturned in a split second and its paddling party scattered liberally along the sides of the gorge.

No previous experience of rafting is required to join any of the trips, which can be day-long or, if you want to explore the lower, more tranquil reaches of the river towards Lake Kariba, several days. Don't be alarmed, though – you won't be thrown in at the deep end. Qualified raft guides provide thorough training and instruction before you depart.

If you need to calm frayed nerves, and have enough energy left after all this adventure, it is well worth hopping on board an upstream cruiser for a sunset wildlife safari. Meandering through the calm and sedate waters of the upper Zambezi, it is hard to imagine how wild the river gets after the Victoria Falls. But keep your eyes peeled – you may just have some close-up encounters with hippos and crocodiles. It seems that even here, on tranquil waters and sipping wine, the prospect of a swim is less than desirable.

Gentle paddling sections do exist

Experienced guides steer the raft

The flow over the Victoria Falls varies throughout the year, building up from its low point in January to peak flow in June. From June to December the flow starts to drop off again. The river levels also affect the rapids you will be able to run. During the low-water season you can raft rapids 1 to 18, approximately 24 km. In the high-water season only rapids 11 to 23 can be run, approximately 18 km. Most visitors base themselves in the town of Livingstone on the Zambia–Zimbabwe border. If you really want to indulge yourself the quintessentially colonial-styled Royal Livingstone hotel, owned by Sun International, nestles on the banks of the Zambezi, with views down to the thundering falls. All activities can be booked and organized through the hotel's dedicated centre on site.

Flying safari
Skeleton Coast, Namibia

Valley of a Thousand Dunes near the Namibia–Angola border

Remote and untamed, Namibia's treacherous Skeleton Coast, lashed by fierce surf and littered with shipwrecks, is a world apart. The only way to fully explore this immense desert wilderness and its otherworldly mountainous interior is by jumping on board a small plane for a unique flying safari.

Recognized formally as a national park in 1971, this narrow tract of coastal desert, 30 km to 40 km wide and 500 km long, stretches north towards Angola and the Kunene River and southwards to the Ugab River. In between, the 'roaring' sand dunes of the Namib Desert, the Himba tribespeople distinctively swathed in ochre robes, flamingos,

Dawn flight from Purros in Hoarusib valley

ostriches, desert-adapted elephants and massive colonies of sea lions share a vast, uncluttered hinterland.

This is without doubt Africa's loneliest stretch of coastline and one of the world's most notorious to navigate. Impenetrable fog, shallow sandbanks and deadly currents have been the undoing of many a hapless vessel or creature that has come to grief on its unforgiving shores. Alongside the rusting hulls of tugs and liners, strewn for endless kilometres, you will also find the eerie remains of bleached bones, both whale and human.

Departing from Namibia's capital, Windhoek, a flight across the Khomas Highland takes you towards the coast and your first

Himba village in Hoarusib valley

Whale bones on the beach near Cape Cross

shipwreck site – that of the *Eduard Bohlen*, a steamer that ran aground at Conception Bay. Its rusting remains can be spotted partially buried in the sand several metres inland from the present shoreline. The low-level journey continues over Cape Cross, where a huge colony of over one million sea lions, estimated to eat 500 tonnes of fish a day, can be spotted.

Your first experience of a makeshift landing strip comes with the first pangs of hunger. Lunch at the beach flying-safari-style is simply a case of picking your spot. Along with shipwrecks there are the remains of old diamond-mining operations, turning lunch into a serious beachcombing session.

Back on board, and as you head inland, the Ugab formations – an almost lunar-like landscape of dark black ridges, where the Congo and Kalahari plates collided – contrast starkly with the white desert. Further into the wilds, the first camp, at Kuidas, nestles in the Huab valley. A hot shower, a comfortable bed, a three-course meal and a glorious view over the plains await.

In the surrounding hills and caves you will find ancient rock drawings by the San bushmen who once tracked here. In the heart of this expansive valley the remarkable red lava and yellow sandstone of the Huab River formations can be discovered on a four-wheel-drive adventure.

The flying safari continues northwards to touch down at the unique 'roaring' dunes. These occur in a narrow band some distance from the coast, where grains of sand reach a certain critical size. Just the merest contact between the grains and anyone who slides down

Desert elephant in Hoarusib valley

Worled tree in Hoarusib valley

the dunes creates a loud roaring noise, thunderous enough to sound like a World War Two bomber.

Further north the next campsite, at Purros, nestles underneath palm trees in a lush oasis in the Hoarusib valley, where you stand your best chance of spotting a desert elephant. You will also have the rare opportunity to visit a Himba settlement, where you will meet the only tribespeople in Namibia who still live traditionally, in tiny gatherings of adobe huts.

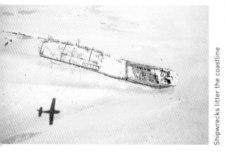

Shipwrecks litter the coastline

Himba women decorate their faces with ochre

Spectacular landscape en route to the Valley of a Thousand Dunes

From Purros you fly over the Valley of a Thousand Dunes towards the Angolan border. Your final camp is on the banks of the Kunene River, overlooking its broad, flowing waters. After days spent among so much sand you may just find you have never been so pleased to see water again – crocodile-infested or not.

ⓘ ··

Measures to preserve the natural habitat of this precious area are strictly enforced and day-trip entry permits for casual visitors are available only for the southern region of the Skeleton Coast Park, between Ugabmund and Terrace Bay. The northern section, between the Hoanib and Kunene rivers, which makes up nearly 70 per cent of the park is strictly off-limits to independent travellers. Skeleton Coast Safaris, a family-run business established in 1977 by Louw Schoeman, the founding father of the national park, provides a wealth of knowledge, expertise and insight on its unique flying safaris. If you have time to explore further, the famous red dunes of Sossusvlei should not be missed. Wilderness Safaris offers a variety of luxury accommodation within easy reach of the dunes. Several airlines fly to Namibia, including Air Namibia, who offer flights via Frankfurt, Germany.

Old mining camp boat

Tracking spirit bears
Princess Royal Island, Canada

Princess Royal Island, a god-given rainforest paradise of moss-laden trees and tumbling rivers, off the west coast of Canada, is one of the few places in the world where you may have the privilege of encountering a spirit bear. And spirit bears are no ordinary bears. Not only do they look unique with their white, or more accurately champagne, colouring – the result of a recessive gene – they also have a prominent spiritual place in the lives of the Kitasoo-Xaixais First Nation people.

Kitasoo-Xaixais longhouse at Klemtu

Spirit bear on Princess Royal Island

Forming part of the Great Bear Rainforest, the largest tract of old growth, temperate rainforest left anywhere on the planet, Princess Royal is a magical, uninhabited island. Think elves and pixies and *Lord of the Rings* film sets, and you may come close to picturing the tangled, mossy web of old trees that makes exploring here possible only on foot.

So few people have been to Princess Royal, and so dense is the rainforest, that at times the only way to move around is to follow the

Final approach by floatplane to Klemtu harbour

best trail-makers on the island: its bears. No, it's not a mistake and it's not crazy, as long as you have an expert guide with you to keep an eye out for imminent encounters. And who better to ask for a guide than the Kitasoo and Xaixais people themselves? They know the land as if it was etched into their souls at birth and have a spiritual connection with the bear everybody wants to see: the spirit bear, or Kermode bear as it is rightly known. They believe it was painted white by the gods in order to remind them of the devastating last Ice Age.

Klemtu on neighbouring Swindle Island is the base for trips to Princess Royal, and if the seaplane or ferry ride there isn't enough to whet your appetite for a watery lifestyle, Klemtu Tourism's cosy, Norwegian-style floathouse accommodation should do the trick. Community owned, and operating since 1996, it is the only tour company that is allowed to track spirit bears. Klemtu itself is a tiny village with a mighty fine longhouse. Recently constructed, this is the pride of the Kitasoo-Xaixais community and is adorned with First Nation art and totems.

Spirit bears are endangered and perhaps only four hundred exist, along with black and grizzly bears, in the Great Bear Rainforest. All types of bear are under increasing threat, and poachers are known to be active, so it is unwise to reveal the exact locations of tracking trips. Suffice to say, it is an incredible experience to sit, heart racing, just 20 metres across a waterfall from a black bear scooping salmon from the water.

Even better is the engaging quest for the spirit bear, which takes you to several parts of Princess Royal Island. Coming across a freshly killed and half-eaten salmon on a forest trail is enough to make you feel you are one corner, or maybe one step, away from coming face to face with one of these champagne-coloured creatures. You will need patience, though, and an acceptance that luck won't always be with you.

Crossing a stream on Princess Royal Island

A Kitasoo-Xaixais longboat in Klemtu Bay

First Nation art on Klemtu's longhouse

For us, during the boat ride up Princess Royal Channel, a favourite haunt of whales and seals, a spirit bear emerged on a nearby beach. Some distance away, it was like a beautiful, serene ghost, ambling along the rocky shore, sniffing here, pausing there. The spirit bear. Majestic and unquestionably special. As it wandered up a river tributary teeming with salmon our guide, Evan, gave us the nod to disembark. We didn't have to go far. Just metres beyond a fallen tree the spirit bear was tucking into its fresh catch. Aware of our presence but unperturbed, it finally sauntered off into the bright green, mossy forest. We breathed again, at once exhilarated and silenced in awe.

ⓘ ....

Many airlines fly to Vancouver, and Canadian Affair offer charter flights from the UK. Princess Royal Island is about 500 km north of Vancouver and cannot be visited independently without a permit as it is Kitasoo-Xaixais territory. First Nation-owned Klemtu Tourism offer fully-guided tours. The only way to reach Klemtu on Swindle Island is via the BC Ferries service that arrives every few days from Port Hardy on Vancouver Island, or by seaplane, which is operated daily by Pacific Coastal Airlines from Bella Bella on Campbell Island. In September the annual salmon run is at its peak and bears come to rivers to gorge.

Spirit bear on Princess Royal Island

Sunset over Klemtu Bay

Fly-fishing and whisky
Inverlochy Castle, Scotland

Fly-fishing on the lower Garry River

There is no better way to immerse yourself in Scottish traditions than at the end of a line, perfecting the art of fly-fishing and sampling a wee dram of whisky at a perfect Highland retreat like Inverlochy Castle, just north of Fort William. When Queen Victoria visited the castle in 1873 she wrote in her diary, 'I never saw a lovelier or more romantic spot'. And she didn't even go fishing.

Scotland is not easily defined. In certain tranquil moments this bold, often uncompromising land of moody lochs, exposed moors and craggy mountains changes before your very eyes. As the day's end gently

sweeps the hillside in a swathe of orange light you may just glimpse its softer side. This is when the rivers, teeming with salmon, can turn into meandering trails of gold as if the water has become whisky.

    As you settle down with just a rod and a wicker basket on the heather-clad banks of a burbling waterway like the Garry River, any frustrations will drift away as gently as the circling water in the eddy pools that make for some of the best fishing. It's just you and the comforting flick and zip of the line, seeking a perfect metronome rhythm. If you are a newcomer to fly-fishing a few hours learning the basics from a gillie may leave you with a lifetime's obsession. He can

Casting at the lochans on the Upper Garry

Beautiful Inverlochy Castle sits below the Nevis range

also help you to refine your cast in order to tempt the fish with a perfectly placed fly. With time, this becomes more than just a sport. For many it is an art form.

There are numerous idyllic places for fishing in the Highlands but the river and loch in Glen Garry are as good as any. Running from east to west, the Garry River flows from the head of Loch Quoich into Loch Garry, which has the village of Invergarry at its western end. Cloaked with Scottish pines and surrounded by Munros – Scottish mountains over 3000 ft (914 metres) high – like Gleouraich and Spidean Mialach, the glen is off the beaten track.

Scotland boasts an array of unique places where you can rest at the end of a long day's fishing, from traditional inns to your very own castle. Set against a rugged mountain backdrop and hidden from view by woodland, the resplendent Inverlochy Castle Hotel has been frequented by royals and rock stars. Close to the site of the original, and now ruined, 13th-century castle, it was built by Lord Abinger in 1863 and remained a private residence until 1969. Recent famous guests have included Sean Connery and Elton John. At the end of a sweeping driveway a turreted entrance leads to chandeliered ceilings, hunting trophies and gourmet delights in the restaurant. For just a short while you can imagine yourself chief of the clan or king of the castle.

Whisky barrels at Ben Nevis Distillery

Dawn over Loch Linnhe near Fort William

The grounds of the hotel are a perfect vantage point to see the grandest of Scotland's mountains. Ben Nevis is the highest of all British peaks, and reaching its lofty (1343-metre) summit is a popular and challenging hike. But it's not just what goes up that matters; what comes down is also pretty special.

More than 900 metres high, on the mountain's north face, nestles an all-important source of water. Captured by the Ben Nevis Distillery far below, this water is the single most important ingredient in their version of Scotland's best known drink: whisky. The production of a good whisky relies upon a pure water source – the name comes from the Gaelic 'usquebaugh' or 'water of life' – and the wonderful wet stuff that flows off Ben Nevis comes from the highest source in the country.

With over a hundred different distilleries in Scotland to choose from, you won't be short of a wee dram wherever you go; another fine reason to get hooked on the Highlands.

River Garry and storm clouds at sunset

Snow dusts the hills around Fort William

ⓘ ....

Inverlochy Castle can arrange the services of a gillie for you. If you are fishing on the Garry River be aware that there can be sudden rises in its water level. The river is dammed high up and releases take place approximately once a week. Accommodation in the Highlands gets booked up quickly in the high summer season and during school holidays, so book ahead.

Traditional gillie fly-fishing gear

Autumn brings the Scottish pine to life

Hiking through arches
Moab, USA

Delicate Arch at sunset

Embedded deep within the Colorado Plateau where it sprawls into Utah, Moab is at the centre of a quintessential North American outdoor playground. Set in a desert-like arena of deep canyons, natural rock arches, white-water rivers and imposing sandstone towers, it boasts access to a unique collection of otherworldly landforms. Although there is no shortage of activity options, the easily reached and expertly managed hiking trails of the Arches National Park offer the best snapshot of this grand, spectacular landscape.

Hikers in Turret Arch opposite the Windows

A small, laid-back town near the eastern border of Utah, Moab attracts a pilgrimage of mountain bikers, hikers, rafters and rock climbers from around the planet. But you don't need to be an adrenalin junkie to have fun. With both Arches and the expansive Canyonlands National Park – a more demanding hiking choice – on its doorstep, Moab can accommodate anyone looking for a dose of outdoor vitality.

With more than two thousand arches exquisitely crafted, over 100 million years, by water, ice, subterranean salt movements and

extreme temperatures, Arches has the highest density of natural, rock arches anywhere in the world. Before entering the park it is wise to stop at the visitor centre where the staff can advise on the best trails to explore. No single hike takes more than a day, and several take no more than an hour or so at the most, but there are many trails worth exploring so don't expect to see everything in one visit.

Hiking around gravity-defying Balanced Rock

The drama begins to unfold within the first 1.5 km of the 74-km drive around the park, at Courthouse Towers. Most of the rock formations visible there today are formed from a layer of salmon-coloured Entrada sandstone deposited during the Jurassic period (between 144 million and 208 million years ago). There can be no better introduction to the human-dwarfing scale of what lies ahead than this wilderness of giant monoliths and monumental slices of sandstone.

View through the arch of North Window

Driving through Arches National Park

Ute Indian petroglyphs, near Wolfe ranch

Beyond a sea of petrified dunes that ripple away towards the La Sal Mountains, the park road reaches the gravity-defying formation Balanced Rock. Standing 39 metres high, the precariously perched, oversized boulder atop a narrow stem seems a mere breath away from toppling. A 550-metre hiking trail loops around the rock, below which it is impossible to feel at ease!

A favourite formation is the Windows Section. Looking like the openings in a giant's eye mask, the mature arches of North Window and South Window are 15 to 18 metres high and about 30 metres wide. Opposite the Windows is the impressive Turret Arch. Eroded from a weirdly shaped, stand-alone rock outcrop – with a turret, of course – the high arch is perfect for wandering through.

Further north lie the most challenging hikes: the 5-km trail up to Delicate Arch and the labyrinth of trails collectively known as the Devil's Garden. The latter, with the 93-metre-span Landscape Arch one of its highlights, will keep you entertained for at least half a day, or a full day if you take the more strenuous but highly recommended 'Primitive Loop'. Stacked stones mark this trail.

If you only do one hike here, make it the one to Delicate Arch. At the trailhead is the abandoned Wolfe ranch, all that remains of the attempt by Civil War veteran John Wesley Wolfe to settle the area in the late 19th century. Don't miss the Ute Indian rock carvings up a short track behind the ranch. Beyond the ranch, the trail winds through cuts and canyons before climbing a smooth rock slope to a narrow ledge.

Without warning you emerge on to the rim of a deep and swirling sandstone bowl, gracefully crowned by Delicate Arch. Even Henry Moore would have been hard pressed to sculpt such proportions and sinuous elegance. Sit down, relax and watch the sun go down across the sumptuous curves, canyons and spans of this extraordinary landscape.

ⓘ ....

Take drinking water, even on short hikes, as it can get extremely hot. There are basic camping facilities within the Arches National Park, but Moab is so close it is easy enough to overnight there. To see Canyonlands National Park from the air, take a thrilling, scenic flight. SlickRock Air Guides operate flights from Canyonlands airport, about 27 km north of Moab on Highway 191.

Sandstone hiking up towards Delicate Arch

Courthouse Towers at the entrance to Arches

Tasting warrior life
Khentii, Mongolia

Just the word Mongolia is enticing, conjuring images of a wild place, wild people and wild horses. And this beautiful country of vast empty steppes, where camels, yaks and nomadic tribes wander freely, is quite unlike anywhere else. Now sandwiched between Russia and China, in the 13th century Mongolia was the largest and greatest empire ever known.

The best way to get a feel for how the hardy Mongols became the most powerful nation in the world under the leadership of Genghis Khan (Chinngis Khaan) is to sign up for a warrior experience in the Khentii Mountains, just to the north-west of Ulaan Baatar.

Late afternoon riding in the Khentii Mountains

Famous bowmaker and archery teacher, Batmunkh

Herding wild Mongolian horses with lasso

Officially titled 'Chinngis Khaan Warrior Training', this adventure should not be mistaken for a 10-day boot camp. By the time you have finished you will be versed in age-old arts like bow-making, taught by legendary characters like Batmunkh, one of only seven bow-makers in all Mongolia. You will learn about traditional vodka distillation, skills like archery, horse herding and lassoing, and the tactics and campcraft of Mongolia's famous warlords.

Living like a true Mongolian nomad in a *ger* (traditional felt tent) and travelling across the country's vast plains and through the inspiring Khentii Mountains on horseback feels like a rare privilege.

Out here there are no restaurants, flushing lavatories or television. Life becomes very simple very quickly, and it feels wonderful. The passing-out parade is one final ride on horseback through a landscape hopefully blessed by the Mongolian Spirit of the Blue Sky, the warriors' favourite deity.

Chimney and roof in a traditional ger

Wooden effigy of Genghis Khan at ger camp

Horses have been central to Mongolian life for centuries. In Mongolian there are more words for these animals than for anything else, and Mongols even drink mare's milk, a salty, sour, fermented concoction. Indeed, horses were the backbone of Genghis Khan's army, bringing speed and surprise to the battlefield. His communication system was also equine based. Messengers rode vast distances along a network of outposts where fresh horses were always available.

Bowmaker Batmunkh's quiver of arrows and hand-crafted bow

Dusk light across the Mongolian steppe

Genghis's soldiers' riding skills, such as the ability to fire bows backwards at full gallop during fake retreats, became legendary and today archery is one of the 'three manly sports' – the other two traditional national games are wrestling and horse racing – celebrated at annual festivals like Naadam.

When it comes to learning to control and understand one of the country's horses yourself there can be no better teacher than a Mongolian horseman. Mongols are perhaps the most natural riders in the world. You can see a fearlessness in them, a gusto and daredevil spirit as wild as the animals themselves. To be a great horseman in Mongolia is to be a great man.

Warrior training involves total commitment – right down to the clothes you stand up in. Mongolians believe our modern outdoor clothing sounds strange to their finely tuned animals. So, to ride a Mongolian horse you first need to dress like a Mongolian.

Traditional dress, still widely worn, consists of a *del* (long padded gown) – a cross between a housecoat and a dressing gown. Felt for men and silk for women. Around your waist goes a silk cummerbund and on your feet a pair of leather boots. For Buddhist Mongols, the upturned toes of the boots prevent any unnecessary killing of insects. Once you pass the initial stage of embarrassed laughter it is surprising how warm you stay and how comfortable you become. Your transition to nomad has begun.

Warrior training is a true adventure in every sense, though you won't end up fighting anybody unless you fancy a go at Mongolian wrestling techniques. But you will feel the impact of Genghis Khan during this distinctly different and beguiling experience.

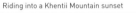

International air travel options for getting to Ulaan Baatar are very limited, with only Air China, MIAT and Aeroflot operating flights. Although you can put together elements of the Genghis Khan warrior experience independently if you have plenty of time, it is advisable to employ an expert operator like Ulaan Baatar-based Nomads Tours and Expeditions.

Riding into a Khentii Mountain sunset

'Lost World' river journey
Angel Falls, Venezuela

'Paradise on Earth' claimed Christopher Columbus when he encountered Venezuela's coastline in 1498. If he had only ventured further inland, what words would he have used to describe Venezuela's richest natural treasure: Angel Falls (Salto Angel), the world's highest waterfall? Words might have failed him even sooner – getting to Angel Falls along the Carrao River, which weaves between a 'Lost World' archipelago of table-topped mountains afloat on a jungle sea, is perhaps one of South America's best wilderness river journeys.

A hiking trail hewn from the rock runs behind powerful Sapo Falls

Set within the Canaima National Park (Parque Nacional Canaima), in the Gran Sabana region buried deep in Venezuela's south-east corner, these bizarre rock islands, or *tepuís*, provided the inspiration for Sir Arthur Conan Doyle's 1912 novel, *The Lost World*. Convinced that their inaccessibility meant there was hope of finding dinosaurs and pterodactyls still alive atop them, he wrote this classic tale that eventually inspired Steven Spielberg's *Jurassic Park*.

To reach the Gran Sabana from Venezuela's capital, Caracas, it is necessary to fly first to unspectacular Ciudad Bolívar. Then the adventure begins, with an exhilarating flight southwards either in a small four-seater plane or an old, silver, twin-prop DC-9 that comes straight out of

the golden age of flying. As you near Canaima, a tiny village populated by Pemón Indians and the base for river trips to Angel Falls, *tepuís* begin to pop their summits through sporadic clouds.

Before departing upriver for the falls, be sure to take the short boat trip and hike to Sapo Falls (Salto Sapo), one of seven waterfalls above Canaima Lake (Laguna Canaima), which you will have seen from the plane. At over 100 metres wide and 20 metres high, the tannin-brown fall is spectacular in itself, but the real treat lies behind

Pemón Indian guides on Carrao River

it: a literally breathtaking path hewn from the rock behind the torrent. The path was cut by a hermit, Tomás Bernal, and traversing it requires a swimsuit – and a dose of courage when you experience the air-sucking power of a massive waterfall.

Although it is feasible to get to Angel Falls and back in a day the pace will be feverish, so if time allows it is better to take a two- or three-day option. Overnighting in a hammock at one of the rustic camps near Auyan Tepuí will add immeasurably to your sense of exploration.

The boats to the falls are driven by experienced Pemón Indian guides, and as the narrow, outboard-motor-powered craft battle against the strong currents of the Carrao, the snaking, jungle-cloaked river plays tricks on your sense of direction. 'New' *tepuís* seem to appear and disappear until it eventually becomes clear that most of them are just one: Auyan Tepuí. Rising above the treeline like an immense, medieval fortress, and turreted with tall, standing, pillar stones, it is a forbidding sight. The name means 'Hell Mountain' and

Auyan Tepui rises above the clouds

Boat on the Carrao River

it is revered and feared by the Pemón Indians, who believe that *marawitón* (bad spirits) live up there with the god Tramán-chitá.

If Conan Doyle had gone looking for dinosaurs he would have been hard pressed to find them on Auyan Tepuí's summit. At a staggering 700 sq. km it is four times as big as Washington DC. Angel Falls launches itself spectacularly from the 807-metre-high plateau in a fine misting, dancing spray.

Missouri-born adventurer, pilot and gold prospector Jimmy Angel brought the first reports of this natural wonder to the outside

Sapo Falls tumbles into Canaima Lake

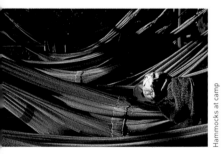

Hammocks at camp

world in 1935. Two years later he deliberately crash-landed his plane, *Río Caroni*, on the summit of Auyan Tepuí and took 11 days to find a way down the treacherous cliffs – a stunt that gave the waterfall its name.

Although Angel Falls can be seen from the river, a short hike towards its base takes you to a far better vantage point. Crane your neck, peer skywards and watch in wonder as the water tumbles down the red rock-face to form the world's highest waterfall.

ⓘ ....

Boat trips to Angel Falls usually operate only from May to November – the wet season, when river levels are higher – but prolonged rainfall may see this period extended. In Canaima and Ciudad Bolívar several airlines, such as Rutaca and LTA, offer flights over the waterfall. National Airline Servivensa offers package tours to Canaima from Caracas, with accommodation in its comfortable Campamento Canaima lodge. Better value can be found with tour operators in Ciudad Bolívar and Canaima.

Angel Falls

Himalayan adventure
Annapurna, Nepal

Porters on the trail toward Machhapuchhare

Ragged rope bridges cross fast-flowing rivers

If only one country in the world were to be given an award for mountain trekking the accolade would surely land at the door of Nepal. With almost four-fifths of the country consisting of the magnificent Himalaya and their foothills, trekking opportunities are limitless and their quality is unrivalled. Selecting one is a matter of personal taste, but for diverse terrain, a reasonable time frame and unspoilt cultural richness it is hard to better the six- to seven-day trek to Siklis in a little-visited region of the Annapurna Sanctuary.

Located in the west of Nepal, the Annapurna region is home to the well-trodden Annapurna Circuit, a highly popular 11-day tea-house trail, but the trek to Siklis should not be confused with this. The six-day adventure is based in part of the

Nepali hill tribe woman walking to market

85

A mountain shrine with spectacular Machhapuchhare in the background

Annapurna Sanctuary, which is protected by the Annapurna Conservation Area Project (ACAP) and was closed to trekkers until the late 1990s. It involves camping rather than tea-house stopovers, which allows access to more remote areas.

The undoubted natural star of the journey to Siklis is the sacred peak of Machhapuchhare, or Fish Tail Mountain. At 6997 metres, it is nowhere near as high as the big-gun peaks of Nepal, which soar to over 8000 metres, but it is the most sacred. So sacred, in fact, that mountaineering on it is banned. From certain angles it is possible to see how the twin rock-fins at its summit resemble an upturned fish tail.

The trail initially crosses a series of rickety bamboo bridges as it skirts the east bank of the rapidly flowing Seti River. It then zigzags up to the tiny village of Ghachok, an ideal place to set up camp below the flanks of Machhapuchhare as they redden in the dusk. Without the

Lamjung massif seen from the high camp at Siklis

Dropping down the trail from Siklis to the Madi River

sun, the temperature in the valley soon plummets and a plentiful three-course dinner *à la trek* is just the ticket for warming you up.

After an altitude-disturbed sleep the customary arrival of a hot cup of tea from the chef tempers the rudeness of pre-dawn wake-up calls. Early starts are part and parcel of a Himalayan adventure. Another reason to poke your head out of your sleeping bag first thing is to see the dramatic sunrises Nepal seems to specialize in.

Easing ever upwards, the route passes nomadic herders, girls carrying unfeasibly large loads of firewood and occasional troops of playful monkeys. Winding through the cobbled-street villages of Chaur and Ghalegaon you encounter the hard-working, unassuming Gurung tribal people. Earning a meagre living from rudimentary agriculture, their existence is substantially improved by their menfolk serving in the British army's legendary Gurkha regiment.

Once height has been gained, after a few tough days of climbing, the trail traverses enchanting rhododendron forests where branches frame the ever-present Machhapuchhare. Eventually, it breaks out across open slopes to reach Siklis. At 1980 metres the village itself is not overly high, but it is backdropped by an awe-inspiring ridge that features 6986-metre Lamjung Himal, and Annapurna II, which is only 63 metres short of the magical 8000-metre height. The trek isn't quite climbing Mount Everest, but the elation of being in the Himalaya is the same.

The route back is spectacular, following the glacial blue, white-water Madi River through villages where fresh mandarins and *lhassi* (buffalo yoghurt) are on offer to refresh weary trekkers. The final camp at Bhagowatitar, an old stone-built village, heralds a chef's cake and a last-night party of singing and dancing. Nepal is about high mountains and snow, but the delightful Annapurna Sanctuary means you don't need to be a mountaineer to be immersed in the Himalaya.

ⓘ ···

There are countless Nepal trekking operators, but the way they operate can differ. Some companies, like Specialist Trekking, which is run by the legendary Himalayan mountaineer Doug Scott, plough their profits back into Nepalese communities. The Maoist insurgency continues to blight Nepal's tourism trade, but so far the rebels have rarely targeted tourists. Check with the Foreign and Commonwealth Office before booking.

Schoolgirls head home in the village of Ghachok

Nepali hill tribe woman with her young son

Whether or not you are an opera buff, a performance of the highly charged, drama-loaded and intensely atmospheric *Aida* is not to be missed, particularly when it's at one of the oldest Roman sites in the world. The open-air Arena amphitheatre, at the heart of the ancient Italian city of Verona, is where this veritable extravaganza of colour, light and sound takes place. If you only see opera once, it should be here.

Aida is performed on a grand scale in the Arena

Cappuccino in Piazza Bra

The whole experience is a celebration of the highest form of story-telling, laced with elaborate details. The basic plot is a good old-fashioned, simple tale of boy meets girl but without the happy ending. Add to this an Egyptian setting and you'll feel as though you've been on a journey within a journey – two holidays for the price of one. The props include a massive, golden, glowing pyramid and

huge sphinxes, while what seems like a cast of thousands further re-creates the glory days of the pharaohs.

Sitting on polished stone steps with only a velvet cushion between you and centuries of Roman history adds a kind of magic to the experience. The pageantry allows a brief glimpse back into a world where the amphitheatre was an entertainment centre of a very different kind. Topping the bill in Roman days would have been struggles between gladiators and lions, before a bloodthirsty, baying crowd.

A trip to Verona need not be just about opera. Indeed, because of its wealth of classical architecture the city is widely regarded as having been second only to Rome in the days of the Roman Empire; and here you will find all the refinement and stylishness of a great Italian city. Immortalized by Shakespeare's most famous lovers, Romeo and Juliet, who were born and died here, Verona now trades as the 'city of romance'. The most popular tourist destination is Juliet's house, complete with balcony – ripe for a re-enactment of the celebrated

Theatrical masks in a Verona market

Egyptian extravagance overflows in *Aida*

love scene. Beyond it, marble-flagged streets, elegant piazzas and attractive, shady narrow alleys can easily be explored on foot.

Getting yourself to the Arena in the morning when the gates open to the public is certainly recommended. The set for the evening's performance will be under construction, and without the crowds you will get perhaps the greatest sense of the massive scale of this remarkable building. Covering an elliptical site measuring 139 metres by 109 metres, it is second only to Rome's Colosseum in size and importance.

At close quarters you can inspect the remains of the perimeter wall, with two rising tiers of rose-coloured arches. Originally, the Arena had a seating capacity of 30,000. Today, with the perimeter wall gone, the Veronese opera season sees it reduced to 15,000 as the rear area of the amphitheatre is taken up by the extravagant stage

Programme seller inside the Arena

WATCHING AIDA

sets. A different opera is performed each night, which means scenery changes every day. The sight of a crane wielding a sphinx or pharaoh high above the city will be enough to stop you in your tracks.

As the time of the performance grows closer crowds begin to congregate in Piazza Bra, the cobbled central square in front of the Arena, and the fashionable and not-to-be-missed business of promenading begins. The surrounding pavement cafés and restaurants fill to overflowing, and the pre-opera ambience

Italian style and chic are abundant in ancient Verona

Waiters on their way to work in Piazza Bra

mounts as the piazza takes on a new lively character, bustling with anticipation.

As you enter the Arena's gates to find your seat among the masses of people, the slow fading of the sun brings the intimacy of the night sky. And as the amphitheatre lights dip you can join the crowd in holding aloft a flickering sea of lighters, and wait for the first resounding rumble of the Egyptian gong. Opera buff or not, it is hard to imagine any other show with such drama in its story, setting or location. Viva *Aida*!

Verona is built above Roman ruins

ⓘ ....

Reserve a table for pre- or post-opera dining as the restaurants fill rapidly. Seats in the amphitheatre range from the cheapest ones on the surrounding concrete steps to prime, VIP seats in the heart of the Arena. All types have their appeal. The camaraderie of the steps is not replicated in the VIP section. For details about performances of Verdi's *Aida* and other operas go to www.arena.it.

Driving Californian surf
Big Sur, USA

No country conjures up images of driving through spectacular scenery like the USA does. Its dramatic landscapes and open roads create several world-class drives, such as Route 66 and the Big Sur. The former is fine if you are on an eternal holiday, but for a quicker driving fix wind down the windows, load up the rock CDs and opt for the Californian classic: Big Sur. It follows US Highway 1 along the rugged Pacific coastline and is as thrilling a drive as you can possibly pack into a few days.

The highway threads its way down the country's entire west coast from Oregon to California, but it is the 145 magnificent kilometres from Carmel-by-the-Sea to San Simeon that make up Big Sur.

Crashing surf pounds the beach near San Simeon

Rear view of Santa Lucia Mountains

Whatever you do, don't miss the popular sunset crawl when cars cruise the bends as the sky bursts into orange and red, and the ocean becomes mercury blue.

From Monterey, home to a fantastic aquarium, take the scenic Seventeen-Mile (27-km) Drive around the peninsula to quaint Carmel-by-the-Sea. The real Big Sur will still be lying in wait for you, though. Almost immediately after leaving Carmel, Point Lobos, the first of many state parks, will greet you, its jagged promontory acting as a barrier against crashing Pacific waves. Point Lobos is good but the drive gets better.

Soon Highway 1, with its eclectic mix of sports-car drivers, Harley riders and motorhomes, begins to climb above the shoreline with striking views almost beyond the horizon. Despite all this natural

Coastline near Julia Pfeiffer Burns State Park

Driving over Bixby Bridge at dusk

beauty Big Sur's best known icon is the dramatic Bixby Bridge. Spanning high above a plunging canyon, it is backdropped by the Santa Lucia Mountains. The cliffs here are so lofty and imposing that the area's notorious early morning sea fog often struggles until after midday to rise up and over them. Patience usually pays off, so hang around for the views.

After passing Point Sur lighthouse you move inland through the layered, gentle hills of the Andrew Molera State Park – a good spot for hiking and riding. The Pfeiffer Big Sur State Park, named after the family who were the area's first European settlers, warrants a couple of days of exploration. Among towering, prehistoric, coast redwood trees, a network of excellent hiking trails includes the gentle Nature Trail and more demanding mountain escapades to Buzzard's Roost and Pfeiffer Falls. If you are fortunate you may see black-tailed deer or bobcats. If you are extremely unfortunate you may encounter a mountain lion!

Big Sur is not all nature and wildlife, though, and there is a thriving community of artists here. Its favourite son was Henry Miller,

Big Sur sunset over the Pacific Ocean

McWay waterfall in Julia Pfeiffer Burns State Park

Looking north up Big Sur coastlines

US Highway 1 clings to the Big Sur coastline

author of the controversial erotic novel *Tropic of Cancer*. Renowned for his straight talking, Miller spent his final years in Big Sur. He was a painter as well as a writer, and you can see his intriguing work at the funky Coast Gallery and the offbeat Henry Miller Memorial Library.

Arguably, Big Sur's finest coastline lies in the south around Julia Pfeiffer Burns State Park. Here, natural rock arches and islets dot the surf and headlands stretch off to infinity. In the park itself a short trail leads to a picture-perfect cove graced by the 24-metre-high McWay waterfall.

The final stretch to the sea-lion colonies and endless sandy beaches around San Simeon is a gentle comedown from the drama of the cliffs to the north. If the wilderness bug didn't bite you, San Simeon's outrageous and outlandish Hearst Castle awaits. A gaudy fusion of every architectural style of recent centuries, it was the home of the newspaper publisher William Randolph Hearst. As Henry Miller might say, 'Everyone to his own'.

Strolling along the beach at Carmel-by-the-Sea

ⓘ ....

If you can, avoid weekends in the high season when traffic congestion detracts from the driving experience. Hotel accommodation along Big Sur is limited but what there is, such as the Ventana Inn & Spa and Big Sur Lodge, is high quality. Petrol stations are rare. There is one in Big Sur village but the prices it charges are extortionate, so fill up in Carmel-by-the-Sea or San Simeon. For great food and views, you can't beat the Nepenthe restaurant, just north of the Coast Gallery.

Swimming in thermal spas

Golden Circle, Iceland

Iceland is a living geological masterpiece, a peerless volcanic land of dramatic skies, bubbling earth, thundering waterfalls and thermal lagoons. If you want an insight into how the planet was sculpted by the forces of Mother Nature, exploring the Golden Circle, a small but diverse region in the island's south-west, will provide many of the answers.

On arriving at Reykjavik, the sight of the expansive, mossy lava fields that edge its brightly painted suburbs only adds to the suspicion that nobody actually lives in Iceland beyond the limits of its capital city. There may be some truth in this, but what lies beyond Reykjavik is mind-boggling in its raw power and natural beauty. First among

Blue Lagoon geothermal spa is at a constant 34–36ºC

Strokkur erupts at Geysir

equals, Blao Lonia (Blue Lagoon) is a huge, blue-green, geothermal
spa lake that not only offers swimmers a remarkably warming
experience but also throws in the power of healing for free.

Contrasting starkly with the black and green contorted remnants
of a volcanic eruption that surround it, the lagoon is a 45-minute drive
south of Reykjavik. Backdropped by the steaming, fuming chimneys
of a geothermal power station, it is at once dramatic, bewildering and
alluring, as if you have landed on a *Star Trek* planet. The lagoon's
milky azure water, topped off with a layer of mist, is mixed with
cooling sea water, silica mud and blue-green algae, and is as
hygienic as anyone could wish for. It is completely replaced every

24 hours and is a constant 34–36°C. Soft and comforting, it seems to cradle your body as you edge into it. Once the water has eased any tensions, a whole range of spa treatments is available, from massages to face masks. If only every public swimming pool was like this one.

A two-hour roller-coaster drive south of Blue Lagoon along a black, volcanic gravel track first skirts around the 'disappearing lake' of Kleifarvatn. Since 2000, when an earthquake ruptured the ground beneath it, about one-sixth of its water volume has drained away and it is still shrinking today. Further south, the smell of sulphur preludes arriving at the Krisuvik Seltún geothermal area. This is on one of four fault lines that run across the Reykjanes peninsula where underground temperatures reach 200°C. The sulphur stench is

Walkway through Krisuvik Seltún geothermal area

Caribbean blue pool at Geysir

Waterfall above continental divide at Thingvellir

overwhelming, but it's well worth holding your nose for a short hike between grey, bubbling mud pools, fizzing yellow fissures and sizzling green vents.

From Krisuvik a lengthy but fascinating track takes you via Selfoss and Reykholt to Geysir, which gave its name to erupting hot springs everywhere. Strokkur, the most active geyser, is not in a particularly grand setting, among mini boiling pools and a Caribbean-blue mineral pool, but you only need to wait at most 20 minutes to see it surge and bubble its way to a triumphant, gushing column some 25 metres high.

Further north, Gullfoss's awesomely powerful waterfall is all the more dramatic because you can't even guess it is there until you are almost upon it. Carved out of a plateau by the torrents of the Hvíta River, it tumbles 32 metres over two tiers into a deep, narrow canyon. Spray mushrooms upwards and on sunny days you may get to see rainbows over the falls. Don't forget to take a waterproof jacket!

Wild Icelandic horses in mountains near Thingvellir

Tectonic divide at Thingvellir

A stunning drive through mountains inhabited by small but tenacious Icelandic horses takes you to Thingvellir, one of the country's most enchanting places, on the shores of Iceland's biggest lake, Thingvallavatn. It was here that the world's first national assembly or parliament was held in 930. Thingvellir sits along the very edges of the Eurasian and North American tectonic plates and they are grinding apart at the stately pace of 2 cm a year. A 40-metre-wide rock chasm, laced with waterfalls, is quite literally the meeting place of continents.

ⓘ ....

Flying to Iceland has become far more affordable. Icelandair offers direct flights to Reykjavik from many parts of Europe and the USA. If you hire a car, check which tracks you can drive it on. As a general rule you cannot travel on F-number ones unless you have a four-wheel-drive vehicle. Blue Lagoon is only signed in Icelandic on approaching roads. The spa is open from 10 a.m. to 8 p.m. in winter (1 September to 14 May) and from 9 a.m. to 9 p.m. the rest of the year.

Green moss cloaks mountains en route to Kleifarvatn

Helicopter flights give a great view of the Strip at night

Big, brash, bright and loud, Las Vegas is the undisputed gambling
capital of the world. No matter what your feelings are about gambling
and big cities, this neon-lit, desert monument to human ingenuity,
unbounded imagination and limitless budgets simply has to be seen
once in a lifetime. Even if it is just for a night, and even if you don't
gamble a cent.

Although it is popular to fly to Las Vegas's international airport,
driving in to the city on Interstate 15 highlights what makes it unique.
Its location in the vast Mojave Desert can only be grasped from afar.
The Great Basin opens up in front of you with the distinctive Vegas
skyline punching up from the desert floor. The impact is massive.

Once the city has a grip on your senses it does everything in its
power not to let go. A walk down the Strip, the main part of the Las
Vegas Boulevard where most of the megaresort casino-hotels
are found, will have you spinning. Megastars of rock, pop and
entertainment flash across gigantic TV screens advertising their
shows, while sphinxes, pyramids and giant golden lions stand

Drive through Little White Chapel

Sunrise over Las Vegas and Mojave Desert

alongside the Eiffel Tower. It is immediately exhilarating, like going round the world in 80 minutes. And luckily even the best hotels, some of the biggest in the world, offer fantastic room rates.

There is so much to see in the city that you need a few days only to scratch the surface. But if you are on a one- or two-day mission, try not to miss a visit to the New York-New York casino-hotel with its replicas of the Empire State Building, the Statue of Liberty and its roof-top roller coaster. The Egyptian-themed Luxor at the north end of the Strip is a towering, black glass pyramid guarded by a gigantic white sphinx, while the Venetian boasts a fully working replica of the canals and bridges of Venice. Take a gondola ride and be sung to, albeit with an American accent.

Another mind-boggling casino-hotel is Caesars Palace, host to many a world heavyweight boxing championship. These days you can skip the bloodshed and watch international stars like Celine Dion. It also features the city's best shopping mall – a fabulous re-creation of Rome, with the Trevi Fountain, colonnades and richly decorated ceilings.

The cloak of night enables the city in the desert to come into its own. Innumerable slot machines, roulette wheels and card and craps tables see feverish activity, and a staggering amount of cash changes hands. On average every visitor to Vegas leaves about $350 lighter. You may win big occasionally, but the casinos are always on top – period.

If gambling doesn't grab you there is a host of free attractions. Top of the list, and a definite don't miss, is the extraordinary Freemont Street Experience in the revamped downtown north of the Strip. This pedestrianized street is covered by a 422-metre-long arched canopy that houses more than 2 million coloured lights. Every night, on the hour from 8 p.m. until midnight, a fantastical, animated light-and-music show dances across the canopy booming out classic hits like Diana Ross's 'Stop in the Name of Love'. Its exuberance is totally infectious and engrossing. Other free casino-hotel shows

Harrahs casino on the Strip

Freemont Street Experience in Downtown

Slot machines are everywhere in Vegas

New York-New York casino with rooftop roller coaster

Giant sphinx entrance to Luxor

worth catching are the exploding volcano at the Mirage and the Bellagio's water-fountain dance.

For a good view of the city head up to the unmistakable Stratosphere Tower. At the top of this 108-storey spike a revolving restaurant and the world's highest fairground rides will thrill you. Do the rides before you eat!

You will either love or hate Las Vegas, but you won't be indifferent to it. And if by chance you fall in love in the city you can always end the trip with a drive-through, Elvis-themed wedding for less than $100. This might be the best gamble of all.

ⓘ ···

There are so many hotel rooms in Las Vegas that there is almost always a deal to be found. So don't be tempted by the more modest hotels until you have checked rates at the fancy ones. For more information go to www.visitnevada.com. Taking photographs in casinos is prohibited – a rule enforced for security reasons. The volcano at the Mirage and the dancing fountains at the Bellagio burst into life every 15–30 minutes in the late afternoon and early evening.

A quarter-scale Eiffel Tower graces Paris casino-hotel

The mere mention of Nepal inspires thoughts of the imposing heights of the Himalaya, where the Earth's skin crumples starkly up towards the heavens along the country's northern edge. Yet there is another, lesser-known, side to Nepal: the south side, along its border with India, where the snow- and icebound mountains melt away into the subtropical landscape of rice paddies, river plains and forests known as the Terai. It is a far gentler landscape to travel through, more Indian than Nepalese, and yet perhaps neither. Inhabited by the unique Tharu tribal people, it is also home to one of Nepal's most enchanting and least expected natural treasures: the Royal Chitwan National Park – a veritable wildlife paradise.

Sunrise over boats on a Rapti River tributary

Inside the park, elephants are the de rigueur form of transport, crocodiles line the banks of the Rapti River and its tributaries, and rhinos, leopards and tigers lurk in the long grasses. Tigers, far more than the distant peaks of the Himalaya, will dominate your thoughts during your time in Chitwan, even though sightings are rare. Whether you long to see a big cat, or fear coming close to one, there is an exhilaration in following trails through the dense forest and high grass knowing that one may be nearby. Hence an instant appreciation of the elephant transport system and its relative safety. Tigers know the

Riding elephants
Chitwan, Nepal

Elephant ride through the dawn mist

futility of messing with these giants, which weigh up to 5 tonnes. Never trust a black rhino, though – best stay atop the elephant, which at least will act as a substantial air bag if one charges.

Established in 1973 by the then king of Nepal, Birendra Bir Bikram Shah Dev, the 1400-square-km park came into being just in time to bring to an end a devastating history of royal hunting and illegal poaching that had left the tigers and rhinos in danger of extinction. In 1938 just one hunt, attended by Lord Linlithgow, viceroy of India, bagged 120 tigers, 38 rhinos, 27 leopards and 15 bears. There were only about a hundred rhinos by 1968 and a mere 20 tigers in the 1970s. Numbers have recovered slightly and the latest estimates stand at about four hundred rhinos and 80 tigers.

In 1984 Chitwan's importance as a surviving 'island' memory of how wildlife-rich this region of Nepal used to be was recognized by UNESCO, who granted it World Heritage status. This has helped to keep at bay, at least temporarily, the impatient and predatory human encroachment and development that encircles the park.

Nowadays tourists come in increasing numbers, but they do not overwhelm Chitwan's wildness. The park stretches east–west, in the shape of an elephant's trunk, along the southern bank of the Rapti River and is usually accessed via the village of Sauraha. This is the base for cheap hotels, lodges and government-owned operators of elephant rides. If you can afford to avoid it and instead stay in one of the six ecolodges inside the park, do. The lodges keep their own elephants and generally care for them as though they are family members, introducing them to visitors by name. Charming but rustic chalets, many lit only by candles, add a welcome touch of luxury to the experience.

With elephants available at almost any time of the day, and experienced phanits to drive them, there is the opportunity to explore at whim rather than being chained to a schedule. This is an essential ingredient, because if there is one way to truly savour Chitwan it is to sit atop a lone elephant, swaying to the rhythm of its slightly graceful, slightly lumbering steps, in the ethereal light of dusk or dawn. At

Terai village

Moonrise over the Terai

Tall grasses can hide rhinos and tigers

times, especially around first light, a fine, backlit mist enwraps the rivers, grasslands and riverine forests, devouring sounds and adding to the primeval ambience. Spotting the silhouette of a black rhino, and silently edging closer to it merely at the tugging behest of the phanit on the elephant's ear, is as close as you can come to prehistoric hunting without endangering the prey or yourself, or needing the kill for food. The freshly cooked rice, curry and vegetables, among other things, served up for lodge dinners ensures you don't go hungry.

The phanit–elephant relationship is a long and trusting one built up from the very earliest years of the elephant's life. However, even a phanit's care is not sufficient to look after this demanding animal and a mahout helps to wash and feed it. The latter is a major task in itself. In just one day, thanks in part to its poor digestive system and large energy-sapping size, a healthy elephant can consume 300 kg of grass and 20 kg of *kuchi* (rice and molasses), and guzzle around 200 litres of water. With such an appetite it is amazing that it can float, let alone swim, but elephants are surprisingly graceful in water.

Terai tribal woman picking crops

A phanit brings an elephant for a dawn ride

Black rhino

Chitwan's myriad animal species are most active at dawn and dusk. It is not just the 'glory' creatures that are worth looking out for. The park is home to large sambar deer, langur and rhesus monkeys, giant flying squirrels and wild boar. If this isn't enough to woo wildlife lovers, Chitwan also happens to be a world-renowned birdlife sanctuary and contains about one-twentieth of all the planet's known species. Ibises, eagles, ospreys and the ever-loving ruddy ducks, which mate for life, are frequent visitors.

In Nepal it takes quite something to tear your attention away from the snowbound peaks of the Himalaya on the hazy northern horizon, but a few days in Chitwan turns them into little more than a sideshow.

ⓘ ....

Fly from the Nepalese capital, Kathmandu, to Bharatpur or take the long but dramatic bus ride from Kathmandu, along the banks of the wild Narayani River and through the heart-stopping Kali Gandaki gorge. The best time to see tigers is after the grass-cutting period in January, when the local people are allowed into the park to harvest the grass in compensation for being removed from the area when the Royal Chitwan National Park was established.

Elephant's eye view of a black rhino drinking

Heli-hiking in the Rockies
Golden, Canada

Stretching almost the entire length of western Canada and the United States, the Rocky Mountains range is a beguiling wilderness of rock, ice, forest and meadow – and a heli-hiking utopia. This exhilarating way to access the high mountains has opened up areas, like those surrounding Golden in British Columbia, that were previously reserved for committed, gear-lugging mountaineers with unfeasibly long holidays. Now, though, heli-hikers can pack a daysack, stay at one of a handful of remote, luxury mountain lodges and wave goodbye to exhausted bodies, damp tents and drab camp food.

View from Purcell to the Beaver Valley and Selkirk Mountains

In the Rockies just about the only things that come in small sizes are the towns. Golden, some 143 km west of Banff in the Rocky Mountain Trench, is a friendly hotchpotch of timber industry and outdoor tourism. The latter is thanks to it being overlooked by Kicking Horse, Canada's latest hot spot for downhill powder-skiing, and surrounded by no less than six national parks. It is also the base for Canadian Helicopters, who operate twice-weekly shuttle flights to Purcell Lodge, an award-winning, low environmental impact lodge set above the Beaver River on the edge of the Glacier National Park. Safe the

helicopters may be, but dull they are not. Swooping over knife-edge, ice-clad ridges and soaring alongside ragged granite summits en route to the lodge, a ride in one is the only way to ascend 1200 metres through mountain terrain in less than half an hour and still be grinning.

Some heli-hiking operations fly into the high mountains several times a day, moving clients from one ridge to another, but others, like the one based at Purcell, prefer to retain a sense of peacefulness by limiting flights. The four-day minimum stay at the lodge also means you are forced to slow down, chill out and absorb the wildness of this pristine environment. And what an environment it is. Set in the alpine zone above forests of subalpine fir and Engelmann spruce, it is home to both grizzly and black bears, who can occasionally be seen roaming the meadows, searching out berries – they can eat 200,000 a day each – and digging for ground squirrels.

Purcell Lodge and the Selkirk Mountains

Late fall snow makes for perfect hiking at Purcell

The ice-clad spike of Mount Sir Donald dominates the Selkirk Mountains

A spectacular helicopter ride provides the only access to Purcell Lodge

To the west, across the deep Beaver River valley, lie the starkly contrasting, serrated, glacier-laced Selkirk Mountains dominated by the 3277-metre pyramidal, black granite spike of Mount Sir Donald. Despite the line-up of other 3000-metre peaks, it is 'Sir Donald', as locals reverently know it, that best captures the high-mountain drama of sunrise and sunset. It may be bitterly cold at dawn, but don't miss peeking your nose over the balcony to see the red morning light slide down Sir Donald's impressive east face on to Illecillewaet Glacier. The same east face also serves as a distinguished navigating marker during hikes.

A real attraction of heli-hiking in this part of the Rockies is the network of all kinds of trails. With encouraging names like Kneegrinder, Roller Coaster and Long Overdue Ridge, they offer hikes for people with just about any level of ability, from day-long expeditions up Copperstain Mountain (2606 metres) and Moonraker Peak (2850 metres) to gentle, short strolls. So you can explore the beautiful landscape, perhaps see a bear and still get back to Purcell in time for afternoon tea and cakes in front of the lodge fire. Don't spoil your appetite for the gourmet dinner, though.

Although heli-hiking is most popular in spring, when wild flowers cover the meadows, and summer, the Purcell terrain also makes for sublime winter hiking in late autumn – snowfall allowing. The real onset of winter sees a change of sport as hiking boots are packed away and skis are dusted off. With an impressively high average snowfall and dry air conditions, the hiking trails become outstanding, deep-powder trails for skiers. The lodge stays open, the helicopters keep flying and the appeal of the sauna increases immeasurably. Whatever season you choose, heli-hiking is simply one of the best mountain experiences to be found on the planet.

Knife edge ridge en route to Purcell

Frozen subalpine fir bark

ⓘ ....

Golden is on Trans Canada Highway 1 between Banff and Vancouver. The nearest international airport is in Calgary, Alberta, about three hours' drive east and is served by several airlines, including charter flights by Canadian Affair. Reduced weight limits for luggage are strictly enforced for all heli-hiking flights so pack with restraint. Purcell Lodge offers a range of summer heli-hiking and winter skiing packages.

Sunset storm clouds over Mount Sir Donald

Felucca down the Nile
Aswan, Egypt

No river can rival the Nile for conjuring up exotic images from ancient history, mythology and a great civilization – and there is no better way to explore it than aboard a felucca, one of Egypt's traditional sailing boats.

Many worthwhile taster trips of an hour or more are on offer in Luxor, but the most enchanting journey is the three-day one from Egypt's southernmost city, Aswan, northwards to Kom Ombo. It is peaceful, less commercial than Luxor and gives you a chance to see a rural lifestyle along the Nile that has changed little in centuries.

Gentle winds mean feluccas have to zigzag down the Nile

Children playing in the Nile near Kom Ombo

Life on board the felucca is not luxurious, with only very basic cooking facilities and shore-based bathroom stops on request. However, this simplicity lends itself perfectly to connecting you with the river and its history, and to living life around the rising and setting of the sun. Waking up on deck as the dawn light begins to paint its deep-blue and orange magic across the previously star-strewn Egyptian sky is more memorable than waking in any five-star hotel room. So, if you are going to 'rough it' just once in your life, this journey should definitely be on your shortlist.

A felucca chef helps to raise the sail at sunset

Life on board is simple and relaxing

The world's longest river, the Nile stretches for 6825 km, from Lake Victoria in Tanzania to its delta on Egypt's Mediterranean coast, and is historically entwined with the country's very existence and subsequent development. As the Greek historian Herodotus said: 'Egypt is the gift of the Nile.' Each year it floods and deposits the life-giving silts that allow crops to grow along a narrow riverside strip in the otherwise inhospitable desert. The Nile was so revered that almost all Egypt's ancient temples were built along its banks, from those at Abu Simbel, south of Aswan, to the great temples around Luxor and the pyramids at Cairo.

Feluccas, with their high, white, canvas sails, originally transported goods up and down the river, but these days they are almost exclusively used for tours. Each one has a captain and a cook, leaving you free to stretch out on a deck mattress beneath a sunshade and chat to the handful of other travellers while you soak up views of life along the Nile. Donkeys are brought to the river to be washed, crowded ferries cross it to connect towns divided by its waters and, as the sun goes down, faithful Muslims pray on its banks. Tiny, thatched-roof villages come and go. And all along, there is the gentle, barely discernible flow of the Nile, combining with whatever wind the day brings to ease you northwards. There are few journeys that are more relaxing – simply because there is little else you can do but relax.

Each night the felucca is moored at an isolated spot on the river bank, and the cook gets to work on his tiny stove. After dinner is the time to stretch your legs on shore, and to sit around the campfire listening to the captain singing songs and telling tales. With so little man-made light pollution in the region the inky, dusk sky slowly develops into a star-show of dazzling proportions. It is easy to see why the ancient Egyptians were so fascinated by astronomy and the movements of the planets. With the water gently lapping at the sides of

Entrance to Temple of Horus at Edfu

Kom Ombo is home to the Temple of Horus and Sobek

the felucca, it is finally time to settle under blankets or into a sleeping bag (it does get chilly at night) for a sleep of a thousand dreams.

Given strong enough southerly winds, you may be able to travel all the way to Edfu, site of the impressive Temple of Horus; dating from the third century BC, this is one of Egypt's finest and best-preserved temples. However, most three-day journeys culminate at Kom Ombo, home to another temple to Horus – and to Sobek, the crocodile god. Wherever your journey ends, you will be reminded of the awe-inspiring civilization the Nile brought into being – a fitting finale to your intimate encounter with this legendary river.

Sunrise over the Nile

(i) ....

Many airlines fly daily to Cairo. Egypt Air flies to Cairo, Luxor and Aswan. Experience Egypt offers an excellent, tailor-made service and will organize your felucca journey. It can also arrange extensions to stay in Luxor, and in Cairo to visit the pyramids. There are countless felucca operators offering tours in Aswan and Luxor, but standards vary considerably. For trips longer than a few hours, you should at least check that your felucca has a sunshade over the back deck.

Waking up on board at dawn

Feluccas were traditionally used to carry goods

Climbing a volcano
Pacaya, Guatemala

Pacaya erupts spectacularly into a moonlit dusk sky

Climbing Pacaya in the afternoon is best to see it erupt

Seeing a volcano erupt is an awesome experience – and in southern Guatemala you can really feel the heat by climbing to the summit of Pacaya (Volcán de Pacaya) for a spectacular close-up view. And no, you don't have to be crazy! There are guided tours every day up this highly active volcano, giving adventurous travellers a chance to see Mother Nature at her most powerful.

Pacaya lies 30 km south of Guatemala City and is an easy drive from Antigua, a beautiful colonial city and now a World Heritage Site. Once the capital of the Spanish kingdom of Guatemala, which included southern Mexico and much of modern-day Central America, it is magnificently surrounded by three dormant volcanoes: Agua, Fuego and Acatenango – all good trek options. Fittingly, given its location, it

Molten lava steams on the flanks of Pacaya

Antigua is a beautiful colonial city

was the power of nature – severe earthquakes have struck Antigua over the centuries – that resulted in the seat of government being shifted to Guatemala City in 1776.

Unlike the newer capital, Antigua has retained its grace and charm, with scores of churches and monasteries mixed in with the colourful, colonial houses along its cobbled streets. It also hosts one of the most elaborate Holy Week festivals around, when entire streets are turned into artworks with multicoloured sawdust-and-flower carpets. The solemn processions and massive floats carried by people are unforgettable in themselves.

No matter when you come to Antigua, you won't be able to miss the Pacaya-tour companies and their leaflet distributors in the Plaza Mayor. But climbing the volcano is no mean feat – it is 2560 metres high, and reaching the summit takes two to three hours of seemingly

Volcanoes surround Antigua and caused it to lose its capital status

Mayan highland tribes come to market in Antigua

one-step-forward and two-steps-back, edging up frustratingly loose, black lava, scree fields. There are two routes up Pacaya and organized groups stick to the easier option, leaving from San Francisco de Sales. Many tour departures are timed so that you arrive at the cone of the volcano in plenty of time for sunset and the full impact of the contrast between the – hopefully – erupting red lava and the darkening sky.

As the hike begins, you hear the slightly ominous, dull thunder-like sounds of eruptions high above. And, just in case you need any more warning that this is not a tour to take lightly, steaming, hot remnants from recent eruptions begin to line the path as you near the active summit: the McKenney Cone. Underfoot, things start to get heated, too, and thick-soled walking boots come into their own. Just as it seems as though you are going to walk over the rim of the cone, the trail turns to the left and up to the relative safety of the old, dormant summit.

On a good day the view from here is awesome. The active vent bubbles and boils, spewing red lava over its sides, and intermittently sends streaming Strombolian volleys of the hot stuff up to 100 metres into the air. The stench of sulphur is all-consuming even if you take care to be upwind of the cone. Beyond Pacaya's breathtaking pyrotechnic show, the conical, silhouetted peaks of Antigua's three other volcanoes provide a stunning backdrop. As dusk heads deeper into the night, the burning red and orange lava creeps down the side of the volcano. For you, too, it is time to descend.

ⓘ

Volcanic activity on Pacaya can be checked at the Inguat tourist office, near the cathedral, in Antigua. Its staff will also recommend authorized volcano-tour companies, such as Eco-tour Chejo's. Ascending Pacaya without a guide is not advised. Some climbers brave going right up to the rim of the active cone, but beware – doing so is a complete lottery as no sequence of gentle eruptions ensures that the next one isn't going to be huge. This is no sanitized tourist experience and it is important to stay very aware of what is going on as you ascend. The Hotel Posada de Don Rodrigo in central Antigua is a unique, colonial place to stay.

Mayan woman and her daughter preparing flowers for sale

Trekking the Milford Track
Fiordland, New Zealand

If you are going to pull on a pair of hiking boots and strap a rucksack to your back just once, New Zealand's Milford Track, hailed as the 'world's greatest walk', has to be the trek to take. Traversing the heart of South Island's dramatic wild fiord country, it winds through native bush and rainforest, glaciated valley systems and up into the high mountains at the Mackinnon Pass. It then skirts majestically downwards past rivers and waterfalls, including the awesome Sutherland Falls, to Milford Sound crowned in scenic splendour by the jagged Mitre Peak.

Dramatic mountains line the trail from Glade House

Milford Sound

Mitre Peak dominates Milford Sound

Ever since Quintin Mackinnon and Ernest Mitchell first pioneered the route in 1888, walkers ranging from hardened trekkers to novices literally wearing their first hiking shoes have been taking up the challenge of this four-day, 53-km trail. And there is an easy and a hard way to do it. Guided walks offer the relative luxury of lodge accommodation, three-course meals, hot showers and a glass of wine at the end of the day. Independent walkers use a system of huts along the track, but are required to carry and cook their own food.

If you join a guided walk your experience begins with a trek briefing in Queenstown after which you travel by coach to Te Anau. Here you board a launch for the head of Te Anau Lake. The boat ride is a memorable approach to the track with mountain vistas rearing loftily in the distance, their edges blanketed in deep forest. When you arrive at your destination it is only a 20-minute stroll along the fern-lined trail to the first lodge: Glade House.

The Wetland Walk is a short detour

Rainforest cloaks the trail near Glade House

On the second day of the trek, a suspension bridge strung across the Clinton River brings the first bit of precarious excitement. The trail then winds through thick, beech forest past Mackinnon's hut to a sidetrack called the Wetland Walk, which takes you through a unique reserve area of protected ferns and mosses. After this you can savour the luxury of some level walking as you follow the old, broad, packhorse trail before climbing into the western branch of the

A waterfall tumbles down a narrow canyon

The trek high point, Mackinnon Pass, is overlooked by Mount Balloon

Wispy waterfall near Pompolona Lodge

Clinton valley – its 1220-metre walls can make you feel incredibly small.

After an overnight stay at Pompolona Lodge you will have to be up at the crack of dawn to give yourself plenty of time for the daunting ascent to the 1073-metre Mackinnon Pass. You cross another wobbling suspension bridge and then the climb begins in earnest, with a series of forested switchbacks. Gradually getting higher you finally emerge to an awesome view of the Nicholas Cirque, a natural amphitheatre at the head of the Clinton valley. One final push, and you will make it up to the pass and the memorial cairn built in 1912 to commemorate Mackinnon and Mitchell's efforts. A sea of jagged mountain tops and deep valley systems stretches far into the distance.

The track follows along the saddle, skirting the edges of imposing Mount Balloon, before descending almost another 6 km to Quinton Lodge. It can be hard going on the rocky and uneven ground, so concentrate instead on the towering cliffs, glacial streams and a pretty boardwalk through a canyon of tumbling waterfalls. If your legs are still up to it, take the 90-minute return walk from the lodge to the Sutherland Falls – which, at 540 metres, stands as the fifth-highest waterfall in the world.

After all the efforts of the previous three days the final stretch will probably seem like a breeze. The track descends steadily, and by the time you reach the 43-km peg you will be back in the rainforest and on fairly even ground. The refreshing sight of Lake Ada means you are close to Sandfly Point, where you can finally hang up your boots. From here, a boat transports you into the majestic, glacially carved Milford Sound. There's no better way to celebrate completing the trail than boarding the *Milford Mariner* sailing boat for a tranquil overnight voyage into the sound to see the sun set over the Tasman Sea. A short walk up on deck will be the only exercise required.

ⓘ ....

A few airlines, including Air New Zealand, fly several times daily to Queenstown, directly and via Auckland. The Dairy Guest House, a converted dairy in Queenstown provides perfect pre- and post-trek accommodation. Guided walks can be arranged through Ultimate Hikes, while the perfect end to the trek is to sail with Real Journeys through Milford Sound on the *Milford Mariner*. For an exhilarating return journey to Queenstown, take a scenic flight for some breathtaking mountain views.

Sunrise catches a peak en route from Glade House

Clambering on to a 'ship of the desert' for a camel trek among Wadi Rum's soaring, sandstone rock islands, which so inspired Lawrence of Arabia, is the ultimate way to see this unique and beguiling wilderness, where silence still exists.

From the fourth century AD, the semi-nomadic Nabataean people ruled all the major trading routes in southern Jordan, including the one through Wadi Rum, where they built temples. Frankincense and myrrh from Arabia-felix (now Yemen), purple cloth from Phoenicia and spices from India made them one of the wealthiest groups in the world. These days, Bedouins descended from the Nabataeans are the backbone of Wadi Rum, and the tribesmen make great guides for any desert adventure, whether it is rock climbing, hiking or camel trekking.

Camel trekking
Wadi Rum, Jordan

Exiting dramatic Barrah Canyon

The Howeitat tribe rules the roost in the popular Rum village and Zweidehs run things in nearby Disi, a quieter, wilder area for camel trekking. From here, it is possible to access the valleys and rock mountains, or jebels, to the east of Jebel Um Ishrin, where vast tracts of unspoilt desert butt on to pockmarked, towering cliffs and giant boulders.

When it comes to bad reputations, camels are near the top of the pile – ask almost anyone, even a Bedouin. They are grumpy, moody and short-tempered, and are not averse to spitting at someone who annoys them. The good news is that their reputations are worse than

Mud flats leading west from Disi

Camels have a habit of spitting – so keep clear!

146

A ride around Jebel Um Ishrin at sunset

the reality. Sure, camels aren't the happiest of animals (unless they're eating) but nor are they looking to unseat you within seconds of your mounting them.

During the first part of the trek, across the flats from Disi towards imposing Jebel Barrah, you will probably be trying to find a comfortable sitting position on the vaguely padded, wooden saddle. Once you have mastered this and settled into the camel's stunted, loping motion, you will be able to look skywards and admire the myriad rock forms that skirt Jebel Um Anfus and Jebel Abu Arashrasha. Up close it looks as though much of the rock is melting, like chocolate, under the incessant sun.

Early departures are best if you want to take a shady break during the oven-like midday heat. They also leave plenty of time to explore. The half-hidden Barrah Canyon is one of the region's most spectacular features, where cliffs close in on you as you squeeze and twist between Jebel Barrah and Jebel Abu Judaidah. The gentle but persistent pace of the camel takes you around the valleys and

Wind-whipped sand dunes near Disi

Sunset over the jebels viewed from near Disi

canyons, and over the dunes, with surprising efficiency – it's possible to travel 40 km or more each day.

While any wildlife is likely to be out at night rather than during the day, the desert is not lifeless. Skeletal tamarisk bushes provide much of the sparse vegetation cover along the valley floors, and high up the twisted roots of junipers slowly search out any available moisture. If you are very lucky, you may even spot the rare ibex. Apart from your companions, the only human life you are likely to see is the occasional Bedouin shepherd moving his herd of goats from one thin patch of desert plants to another. At times, a four-wheel-drive vehicle may buzz past, but not often enough to become bothersome.

Overnight you can camp in a goat-hair tent and enjoy the hospitality the Bedouin are renowned for. While sunrise and sunset are definitely worth catching, it is in the hour or so before the sun rises and after it sets that the light seems to blend seamlessly with the jebels and dunes of Wadi Rum. This is also the time when lasting memories are formed of the silence of the desert – the deafening silence of a truly wild place.

Riding across mud flats near Disi

(i) ···

Royal Jordanian Airlines flies direct to Amman and from there it is a five-hour drive south along the Desert Highway to Wadi Rum. Accommodation options are somewhat limited, with newly developed desert camps like Desert Explorer's Bait Ali camp near Disi offering the best camping comfort in a traditional Bedouin setting. Desert Explorer also organizes camel trekking from Disi, and horse rides in the desert. Camel treks can last from a few hours to several days. For more information, contact the Jordanian Tourist Board.

Partying at Mardi Gras
New Orleans, USA

Festivals don't come much bigger than the annual Mardi Gras carnival in New Orleans. Over a couple of weeks leading up to Lent this laid-back jazz and blues capital dances, struts and parades itself to the infectious rhythms of marching bands. And you can do far more than simply watch it from the sidelines. Whether you are screaming for beads, dancing down Bourbon Street or experiencing the ultimate thrill of riding a Mardi Gras float, this exuberant celebration will sweep you away.

Set along the banks of the lazy Mississippi in southern Louisiana, New Orleans is an intoxicating mix of colonial, wooden mansions, wrought-iron balconies and atmospheric jazz and blues bars. Paddle

Canal Street is a great place to catch all the night-time parades

Bourbon Street is the heart and soul of New Orleans

Zulu Rex, the king of the super krewe Zulu

College marching bands perform at most parades

steamers still negotiate the river, soulful musicians perform in the streets and the rich smell of Cajun cooking pervades the air. Even outside of Mardi Gras, a visit to the city is an unforgettable experience. During the carnival it just gets better.

Although Mardi Gras is not on a fixed date every year, 'Fat Tuesday' is always the ultimate day of revelry. At midnight the partying grinds to a swift halt and the relative austerity of Lent begins on Ash Wednesday. So don't come on the Tuesday and expect to have the full Mardi Gras experience. At the very least arrive the weekend before, when many of the super krewes hold their parades. Krewes are city-based social clubs, some with thousands of members, and they are the heart of the festival. They fund, create and fill the floats, host gala balls and coordinate the extensive parade schedule.

Super krewes like Orpheus, Bacchus, Endymion and Rex justifiably attract much of the attention with their elaborate and lengthy floats, but some smaller clubs perhaps embrace the true Mardi Gras spirit best. The irrepressible Mid-City Krewe is an example – and is also one of the few that allows outsiders on to its floats for the ride of a lifetime. Its parade, themed 'Things We Do for Love', is a glittery affair of multicoloured, foil-wrapped floats interspersed with marching bands and outriders on horseback. Float riders have one

Crowds looking for throws in Bourbon Street

task and one task only: to toss beads, toys, cups and coins – known as 'doubloons'– to as many parade watchers as possible. With over a million people lining the route this is no mean task.

At the start of the parade beads are racked up, costumes and masks are donned, and the floats roll slowly down tree-lined St Charles Avenue, its mansions bedecked in traditional carnival colours of purple, green and gold, depicting justice, faith and power. A non-stop barrage of screams flows forth above a sea of waving hands and an indeterminable number of stepladders – widely used to get above the throng in the hope of attracting more beads. For most revellers, this is what Mardi Gras is all about: plastic, gaudy and virtually worthless beads. The crowds build before the tumultuous finale along Canal Street, the city's main street and the widest in the

Super krewes have elaborate floats and distribute thousands of throws

Bourbon Street is the place to trade beads

world. A four- to five-hour ride on a float will lift you temporarily into the realms of being a rock star on tour, or a sporting hero on a victory parade.

In between parades, the legendary Bourbon Street, in the city's beautiful old French Quarter, comes to life – the Mardi Gras celebration was brought to New Orleans by the French in 1699. Above the dimly lit jazz and blues bars, bearers of bead necklaces fill the balconies, and the crowds below go to great lengths to attract a throw. Day and night, the necklaces rain down and they might as well be diamond ones for the furore they cause. Acquiring them, lots of them, is the key to claiming a successful Mardi Gras. Sounds ridiculous? Go and see. Even the most conservative people get caught up in the bead-gathering frenzy of this memorable street party.

Steamer *Natchez* on the Mississippi River

ⓘ ....

Accommodation in New Orleans is booked up well in advance of the final week of Mardi Gras, so book early. Parade streets are closed before and after the processions, so it is best to find a place to stay along one of the routes, for example at the landmark Pontchartrain Hotel on St Charles Avenue. For more information about visiting New Orleans check out the city's Convention and Visitor Bureau.

Red Sea diving
Dahab, Egypt

Dahab

The chilled-out town of Dahab on the Sinai Peninsula is the scuba-diving gem of the renowned Red Sea. It boasts several world-class dive sites, including the Canyon and the notorious Blue Hole, and a variety of depth profiles that will either ease you gently into the sport or have you reaching for a nitrox rebreather.

Located 85 km north of the far more crowded and well-known diving sites of Sharm El Sheikh, Dahab is backdropped by the dramatic, barren mountains of the Sinai Desert. The contrast between overland

Hard coral near the Blue Hole

and underwater could not be more extreme. All the best dive locations are accessible right off the beach, and walking out of the desert straight into the Red Sea adds to the unique appeal of donning your fins here.

One of the most enchanting sites, the Eel Garden, is just around the corner to the north of the main beachfront strip known as the Lighthouse dive area. This shallow dive of 10 to 15 metres takes you down a gentle, seemingly dull, sand slope. However, stay still for long enough and a swaying forest of eels will emerge from the sand, like a

school of cobras mesmerized by a snake charmer. It is tempting to spend the whole dive here rather than heading off on a further foray to see coral fans and the spiny, but poisonous, lionfish.

Other great dives include Golden Blocks to the south, based in a large and tranquil crescent-shaped bay, and the renowned Canyon to the north. You need every breath of air you can muster for the latter, more complex, dive, so on entering the water you snorkel over coral gardens to the edge of the big wall before giving the OK sign and descending. Below a large rock-head a narrow chasm opens up, and you dive through it into a wider cleft teeming with shoals of glassfish. After negotiating the deepening, dark canyon you return to the entrance with, hopefully, enough air left to do a little more exploring around the rock-head before surfacing.

Most people who come to dive in Dahab want to experience the Blue Hole, a seemingly bottomless chasm carved out of the rock-wall

Final equipment check at the Canyon

Divers waiting to descend at Golden Blocks

Dahab is backdropped by the mountains of the Sinai Desert

nearest the shore. Diving straight into this is not recommended unless you are highly experienced, as the hole quickly drops off to a slope at depths of 300 metres or more – and then drops off to eternity. Memorials on the rocky shoreline to divers who succumbed to nitrogen narcosis while diving too deep sober up even the most confident scuba pros.

The safest and most exciting way to see the Blue Hole is to first take a short trek, laden with air tanks and weight belts, over a low promontory to the Bells. Jumping into this narrow pool in the rocks is good practice for what is to follow. Once you have reached the top edge of the wall a narrow, vertical shaft plunges through the rock, down to around 30 metres. The only way through this is to dive head first into the darkness. For a brief moment, all visuals are lost before a faint glow of light can be seen at the end of the shaft and you pop out of the wall to be greeted by the Big Blue. The slightly unnerving view of the open sea at these depths leaves you with no reference points – just an enticing, deep blue all around you.

From the base of the shaft you drift along a wall of grass corals, and past the odd sea snake or conger eel, to the abundant, colourful corals and shoals of fairy basslets around the saddle into the Blue

Hole. Even when you enter in this more controlled fashion, it is imperative to keep a close eye on your depth gauge to stop yourself being drawn downwards to oblivion.

With so many great dives, and the peaceful beauty of Dahab itself, it would be wise to come here soon, before the shadow of Sharm-like development swoops through this Red Sea paradise.

ⓘ ....

Of the many tour and dive companies on the Red Sea, Experience Egypt organizes dive packages in Dahab, via the excellent Orca Dive Club. Prices are keen and instruction standards are high, so it is an ideal place to take the plunge on an open-water course. The basic qualification, this lasts about five days and allows you to dive down to 20 metres. At the other end of experience, Dahab is becoming a red-hot destination for the burgeoning numbers of Tec divers who do more technical dives and use nitrox rebreathers, which allow them to dive to 80 metres or more. Egypt Air flies direct to Cairo, for transfers to Dahab.

Colourful Pennant butterfly in the coral garden at the Canyon

Riding along deserted Pakiri Beach

Pakiri Beach, on New Zealand's North Island, famously featured in films like *The Piano*, is an enchanting spot to saddle up for the ride of a lifetime. With the wind in your face, and the thunderous sound of hoofbeats in your ears, you can gallop a white horse down what seems like a never-ending expanse of white sand.

Pakiri Beach is on the Hauraki Gulf

The beach is just over two hours' drive from Auckland, on the north-east coast, and it stretches enticingly for 21 km. Hidden from view by rolling dunes and a sea of swaying grasses, it is one of those tucked away, not really on the road to anywhere, kind of places. With just a clutch of small, wood-slatted farmhouses scattered at its edge, there is enough space for you to trot, canter and gallop to your heart's content.

Rides aren't limited to the beach. Trekking routes, cloaked in native bush, wind upwards into the surrounding hillsides. You can brush with giant silver ferns, the national symbol of New Zealand,

Trekking along the Te Kiri Warrior Trail to Omaha

Horses at Pakiri Beach stables

and ride loggers' tracks or the historic trails of Maori warriors. While you won't be able to avoid seeing the abundant toitoi, which looks rather like an overgrown lavatory brush, it's advisable to avoid getting too close to bush lawyer plants – they can spike both you and your horse. In summer the native *pōhutukawas* (New Zealand Christmas trees) that line the beach blossom in a swathe of red.

This is a landscape steeped in a history that extends far back to the original Maori settlers, who fished off the beach with hand-sewn nets and farmed the surrounding pastures. With provisions stowed in a saddle bag, what better way to savour this than by taking up the reins and riding along one of the area's most rewarding trails – the Te Kiri Warrior Trail? A highlight of the journey is the climb above the white sands of Pakiri to Pa, where the lookout fortress of Te Kiri, a former Maori chief of the area, once stood. From here, there are sweeping views across the Hauraki Gulf to the Pacific Ocean and the Little Barrier and Great Barrier islands, otherwise known as Hauturu and Aotea, and to the Hen and Chicken Islands and even Auckland itself.

You will also follow in the footsteps of Taukokopu, the ancient Maori warrior and famous runner who raced between the high points of the coastline, looking for approaching war parties and warning his people of their coming. Part of the trail takes you to the Omaha *marae* (meeting house) of the area's Maori community. Here you can unsaddle, put your horse out to graze in the surrounding paddock and experience a traditional welcome, or *karanga* (calling on ceremony).

The first voice to be heard is that of a woman, calling to visitors to come into the *marae*. Then it is the men's turn to speak, retelling histories and welcoming the guests. Once the speeches are over, the visitors are invited inside and their hosts greet them by touching noses – a ceremony known as the *hongi*. Host and visitor are united by sharing the same breath.

Riding onto Pakiri Beach

Galloping through dunes behind Pakiri Beach

The *marae*, a five-hour ride south from Pakiri, is a simple, modern building situated on a rocky bluff. An overnight stay, huddled in blankets and sleeping bags, may not be the most luxurious experience, but it is special. According to Maori legend, if you sleep well in the *marae* you have been blessed by the spirits. After a few days of riding, fresh sea air and tales of warrior runners, a blessing is guaranteed.

There are a number of horse ride operators on North Island. Pakiri Beach Horse Rides offers fully guided treks run by Laly and Sharley Haddon, direct descendants of Te Kiri, the Maori chief. A variety of rides are available, from one-day trips to overnight and full cross-country expeditions, including the five-day Te Kiri Warrior Trail and the seven-day Great Northern Coast to Coast ride. Accommodation is in a variety of homes, *maraes* and local farms. Air New Zealand flies daily to Auckland.

Walking the Wall

Jinshanling to Simatai, China

Outrageous in scale and visible from space, the Great Wall of China barely needs an introduction. Walking along it inspires visions of steadfast Chinese soldiers and charging Mongol hordes, imperious defence and futile attack. Almost everyone has this on their 'to do' list when they visit China, but you can avoid the milling crowds of walkers by heading for the part that starts at Jinshanling.

Stretching for more than 6700 km across the harsh, jagged mountains and the deserts and grasslands of northern China, from the Shanhai Pass in the east to the Jiayu Pass in the west, the Great

The Great Wall winds its way through the harsh mountains near Jinshanling

Watchtowers line the wall

Wall was built over a period of about two thousand years. The Badaling section is by far the most popular one to visit, but it has been highly restored and this, together with the number of tourists, means it is a struggle to get a feeling for its true nature. For anyone who is reasonably fit, a better option is the 12-km-long trek from Jinshanling to Simatai, where the wall and its surroundings retain an appealing air of ruggedness, raggedness and natural disrepair.

Jinshanling is about 120 km north of Beijing, in the Hebei region, and is serviced by a number of tour operators in the capital, who will drop you off there and pick you up again in Simatai later in the

Building the wall across mountainous northern China cost many lives

View of wall near Simatai

afternoon. Although the wall is visible on entering the Jinshanling gate, it is not until you climb the first flight of steps to look along its snaking, crenellated length that you stop in awe. With contouring mountain ridges as far as the eye can see, every high peak crowned with a hefty watchtower, this gargantuan piece of engineering defies gravity as it rears up then plunges down slopes steep enough for extreme skiing.

Initially a series of separate walls built by warring dynasties during the late Spring and Autumn Period (770 BC to 476 BC), the Great Wall itself dates from after 214 BC, during the Qin dynasty, when most of the existing walls were linked and their overall length extended under the emperor Qin Shi Huangdi. The futility of attacking its 7-metre- to 8-metre-high ramparts, coupled with the exhaustion brought on by traversing the mountains that surround it, must have broken the hearts of many an enemy. Even the notorious Mongol hordes of Genghis Khan (Chinngis Khaan) struggled to breach it before capturing Beijing in 1215. When the Yuan dynasty founded by

Genghis' grandson Kublai, who completed his grandfather's conquest of China, fell in 1368 the Ming emperors went on a massive building spree to strengthen the wall, in particular to try to keep the Manchus at bay during the 16th and early 17th centuries.

At first, when you leave Jinshanling, the wall is in good condition, which helps to warm your legs up for the relentless series of steps that take you from one watchtower to another. At the height of China's power, over a million soldiers guarded the Great Wall against attackers. Looking out from a watchtower at the endless, bleak folds of rough mountainside, it is not difficult to imagine the suffering of enemy soldiers, especially in winter, as they marched or rode from the north for months to mount an attack. With each watchtower placed to give sweeping views, and a series of horseback messengers

Walking to Simatai avoids the crowds of other sections

ready to alert defenders on other sections of the wall, the Chinese had an overwhelming advantage.

As you edge closer to Simatai and start to get a feel – even if it is only the ache in your legs – for the magnitude of this giant, brick dragon, the state of the wall begins to deteriorate. In a couple of areas where it is too unstable for walking, footpaths lead off around the mountainside, giving you the enemy's view of the wall's daunting, towering brickwork.

Above Simatai a modern swing bridge now crosses the river and the more adventurous can take a final ride down to the village on a flying-fox zip wire. It seems a pity, though, to spoil an encounter with one of the world's truly great monuments by making such a sharp exit.

ⓘ ⋯⋯⋯⋯⋯⋯⋯⋯⋯⋯⋯⋯⋯⋯⋯⋯⋯⋯⋯⋯⋯⋯⋯⋯⋯⋯⋯⋯⋯

Many Beijing tour operators offer trips to popular sections of the Great Wall, including Jinshanling. Make sure they allow you enough time, about four or five hours, for an unhurried walk to Simatai. The constant up and down makes for slow progress. Persistent local 'guides' will latch on to you from the start of the wall, offering postcards and books. Ignore them – the route is straightforward and the books are heavily overpriced – and they will eventually look elsewhere for business.

Ruined wall near Simatai

A bridge crossing at Simatai

Walking the wall from Jinshanling to Simatai is surprisingly strenuous

Wildflowers line Samaria Gorge

Hiking on the summit of Gingilos

Dubbed the 'Galapagos' of the botanical world, the Greek island of Crete is renowned for its abundance of unique wild flowers in spring. Tucked away in a small bay on the south-west coast, Paleochora is an ideal base for exploring the island's network of trails. From there you can walk through swathes of colour, and bend to spot rare orchids or delicate lilies, while you follow paths that take you to the ruins of ancient civilizations, along deserted beaches, up dramatic mountains and through Europe's longest gorge. It's a memorable experience whether you are a botany fan or not.

First cut adrift from the surrounding continents about ten million years ago, and finally isolated by the rising Mediterranean Sea, Crete is today the southernmost large island of the Greek archipelago. Its long period of isolation is the reason for its unusually high percentage of endemic wild flowers – around 170 plant species are found only here. Each year new discoveries push this number higher.

Cretan Ebony (*Ebenus cretica*)

While you can walk independently on any of Crete's trails, to really get to know the flowers it is invaluable to go with a botanist, such as Jeff Collman, who specializes in the island's flora. Many plants, like the delicate, endemic skull cap (*Scutellaria sieberi*), are easily missed if you don't have an expert to pick them out for you.

A good trail to start with takes you from Paleochora, on the coast, to the lost-in-time hill village of Anidri, 5 km to the north-east. Here the whitewashed, Byzantine church of Agios Georgios is worth stopping for, with its 13th-century frescoes and walls dotted with purple-flowered Cretan wall lettuce (*Petromarula pinnata*). Above Anidri, through a twist of olive groves, a tiny hill church offers spectacular views over the Mediterranean before a track drops down a narrow gorge, lined with attention-grabbing pink oleander (*Nerium oleander*), to Gialiskari beach and a cooling swim.

Another classic, though longer, walk that also has Paleochora as its base is the coastal route from Sougia, 17 km to the east. A short ferry ride takes you to this delightful, secluded fishing village. The trail starts

Spiny Golden Star (*Asteriscus spinosus*)

Centaurea raphanina

Snow Crocus (*Crocus sieberi*)

Pink Rockrose (*Cistus creticus*)

Descending from Gingilos at the head of Samaria Gorge

Piles of stones, or cairns, mark the trails

in a deepening, tranquil gorge filled with Turkish pine (*Pinus brutia*), where it is possible to find enchanting species such as spiny chicory (*Cichorium spinosum*) with its deftly serrated, blue petals, and fragile, flowered capers (*Capparis spinosa*) high up on the overhanging cliffs.

Roughly halfway through the walk the trail drops from a treeless plateau into a coastal bowl, site of the Hellenic and Roman settlement of Lissos. It is unguarded and little visited, and you can sense how idyllic life was here as you explore a small amphitheatre, the mosaics in a temple to Asklepios, the churches of Panagia and Agios Kyriakos, and the eerie tombs of a Roman necropolis. The route to Paleochora climbs back to the plateau before following the sawtooth coastline with its tempting beaches.

Two of Crete's most famous trails – one up a mountain, the other down a gorge – start from above the village of Omalos, easily reached from the village of Paleochora, in the White Mountains (Lefka Ori). Gingilos (2080 metres) is a pyramidal peak that towers above the head wall of the Samaria Gorge, at 17 km the longest gorge in Europe and the most popular walk on the island.

Ascending Gingilos is the more serious proposition as the route crosses rocky, spectacular terrain, with a natural, rock arch the highlight. A lengthy trudge up zigzags takes you to Linoseli col, and from here the summit is an hour-long hike and scramble. The trek gives you a chance to see some of Crete's hardier endemics, such as anchusas (*Anchusa caespitosa*) and Cretan tulips (*Tulipa cretica*) that only grow at altitude. If this is not enough, on a clear day the views from the summit are astounding.

Old cypress tree on Gingilos

Samaria Gorge and the Samaria National Park are justifiably a UNESCO Biosphere Reserve, and in spring the abundance of wild flowers turns the trail through the gorge from a great walk into a world-class one. Starting from a height of 1300 metres, it plunges 1000 metres down steps through an enchanting pine forest to the base of the gorge. As you continue and criss-cross the river, passing tiny churches and ruined villages, swathes of peonies (*Paeonia clusii*) and white-flowered asphodels (*Asphodelus aestivus*) fill the glades.

After a long and often hot day of walking, the trail-end beach at Agia Roumeli is littered with discarded walking boots and rucksacks as their

Original marble at church in Lissos

owners plunge into the refreshing sea. Discovering wild flowers can rarely be this much fun.

ⓘ ....

Wild-flower walking trips with botanist Jeff Collman, the author of *Walks with Crete's Spring Flowers* (Beechwood Press), are offered by Freelance Holidays. Temperatures can soar, even during early spring, and there are few places to find shade or water on Crete's high mountains. Tourists flock to Samaria Gorge, especially during the peak summer months. Starting out early in the day at any time of year can help you to retain a sense of wilderness.

Finding paradise

Dhoni Mighili, the Maldives

A speck in the Indian Ocean, Dhoni Mhigili is paradise found

If you want to escape to paradise, surround yourself with nothing but ocean views and indulge in spa treatments, secluded Dhoni Mighili, set in the crystal-clear waters of the Maldives, is the island you have been dreaming of.

A tiny speck in the middle of the Indian Ocean – it takes only 800 footsteps to round its sandy circumference – Dhoni Mighili ('boat island') is a dreamy world of luxurious indulgences. With only six bungalows, it never caters for more than 12 guests at a time, so you will have most of its white sands and shimmering turquoise sea to yourself. To get to it from the airport at Male takes either a

30-minute seaplane ride over a necklace-like string of atolls or a four-hour cruise on your own private *dhoni*, a traditional Maldivian sailing boat.

These lovingly crafted, 20-metre wooden boats with double sails have been specially built to allow guests to live on board if they want a change from their bungalows, as well as using them to journey, explore and indulge. With such enticing names as *Sublime*, *Serenity*, *Dream*, *Passion*, *Seduction* and *Bliss* they will take you to visit nearby islands or go snorkelling; or you can simply enjoy a sail, a glass of wine and the chilled-out decadence of lounging on deck on one of the huge, cushioned daybeds.

Spa treatments include 'holistic heavenly bliss'

And the relaxing need not stop when you are on land. You can take a dip in your own private plunge pool, lie back in the shaded garden of your bungalow or simply curl up on an *undholi*, the luxurious, wood-carved swing bed traditionally used by Maldivian families

Throughout your stay you will also have your own dedicated *thakuru* (butler) on hand 24 hours a day, as well as a captain and two crew members, all immaculately dressed in the traditional colourful *mundu* (sarong). The service is 'wherever and whenever'. So if you fancy sailing off into the sunset, or having a land-based candlelit dinner under the stars at midnight, you quite simply can.

Spa foot bowl

For the more adventurous, there's windsurfing, catamaran sailing and kayaking, as well as a dive school if you want to enjoy the Maldives' world-class underwater action. But if you just want to unwind and spoil yourself, the Sen Spa can provide some serious pampering. With indoor and outdoor treatment rooms, both overlooking the sea, it's not difficult to drift off to sleep to the sound of water gently rising and falling.

The spa menu includes the deliciously named 'holistic heavenly bliss', an all-over body treatment that is as good as it sounds, scrubbing, cleansing and polishing your skin so that it feels like new. And after a long flight to the Maldives you may wish to take advantage of the 'jet lag reviver' – or even the hot-stone treatment, which uses

hot, black basalt to restore flagging energy. The tropical fruit wrap, made with fresh fruits including coconut, papaya and pineapple, almost looks good enough to eat.

Wining and dining is definitely a key part of the Dhoni Mighili experience, and with water all around it's no surprise that seafood is a big hit on the menus. Tropical fruits are also in abundance and make any meal truly exotic. Before you arrive you will have been asked about any special requests you have, including food you like and don't like. This means the resident chef can rustle up your favourite dishes at just a moment's notice. When it comes to where to eat you can choose between the restaurant, dining on board your *dhoni* or picking a secluded spot on the beach – some people even ask for their table to be in the water.

Relaxing and unwinding is the easy part of staying on Dhoni Mighili – the hardest part will be leaving the paradise you have found.

Sunset over traditional *dhoni* boats

ⓘ ··

There is a wide choice of operators and resorts in the Maldives to suit a variety of
budgets. Specialist operators Seasons in Style provide tailored itineraries to
Dhoni Mighili. And if you want another unforgettable experience, the company
behind Dhoni Mighili has opened the first-ever underwater spa on Huvafen Fushi
in the North Male Atoll, a 30-minute journey by speedboat from the international
airport at Male, the Maldivian capital. Here you can enjoy treatments and
therapies while watching the amazing underwater world go by.

Souk shopping
Marrakech, Morocco

The vivid colours of its bustling souk, the red of its medina walls, the mingling aromas of a thousand spices and the sounds of story-tellers, fire-eaters and snake charmers make Marrakech the world's most exotic location for bargain-hunting.

For centuries the city has been a renowned trading centre. Berbers and Arabs, nomads and tribespeople from the surrounding Atlas Mountains converged in its chaotic central square, Jemaa El Fna,

Feasting begins at dusk in Jemaa El Fna

while merchants from Timbuktu, Egypt and Europe came to deal in cotton, gold, silver, slaves and spices. Today it feels as though little has changed and shopping remains a reason in itself to visit Marrakech's medina, or old quarter.

A maze of alleyways stretches northwards out of Jemaa El Fna, into the heart of the souk. Tightly packed rows of closet-sized stalls line them on both sides and keen salesmen vie for your attention. While they, like Marrakech's hawkers, once had a reputation for high-pressure sales

tactics, things have changed. Now, thanks to the introduction of plain-clothes tourist police, bartering for arts and crafts is a relatively relaxed affair.

It's almost guaranteed that at some point you will get lost in the souk's twist of shadowy, narrow streets, where the sky is crowded out by overhanging carpets and metalwork or leather displays. With so many tightly packed stalls selling an array of products from traditional babouche (bright yellow slippers) to ornamental ironwork lanterns,

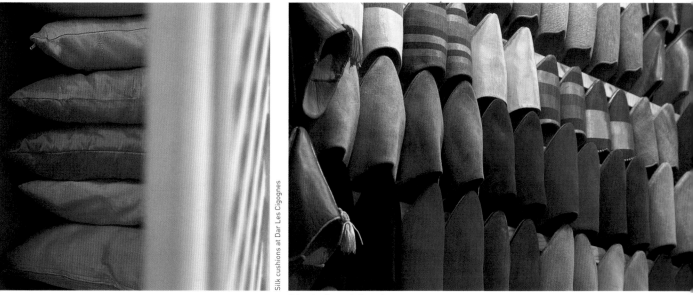

Silk cushions at Dar Les Cigognes

Babouche slippers in the souk

it's easy to let browsing take over and lose your bearings. You will usually find that the next turn brings you back to a familiar spot.

An area not to be missed is Rahba Kedima (the 'old place') off Rue Semaine in the north-east part of the souk, where herbalists tout potions, lotions and spices to cure all manner of ailments or diseases. Here you can pick up black scorpions, bottled leeches and even dried chameleons for medicinal purposes. You may prefer to settle for a simple but effective neck and shoulder massage.

When the hustle and heat of the souk starts to take its toll on your will to barter, retreat to Jemaa El Fna. Its many shady pavement cafés offer refreshing mint tea – or you can try one of the fresh juices from the orange-laden carts that line its perimeter.

It is at sunset that the action really gets under way in the square as musicians, brightly costumed water-sellers, dancers, scribes writing letters, dentists pulling teeth and henna tattooists gather en masse. And shortly after the sun goes down the open-air restaurants take centre stage. Neat, orderly rows of benches, strings of twinkling

Pot-pourri in the souk

Marrakech's souk is bustling with life

lights, tables covered with white cloths and plates piled high with salads, couscous and skewered lamb are promptly assembled, and hazy smoke and enticing aromas fill the air.

The thud of drums and the sound of whining instruments enticing snakes from wicker baskets, street sellers shouting their wares, the hiss of flames and the clatter as snails are cooked in their shells on the food stalls combine in an intoxicating concoction. Although Jemaa El Fna translates as 'assembly of the dead', it brims with life every evening.

Traditional red walls in the medina

Crenellated roof at Dar Les Cigognes

For a more chilled-out view of proceedings, watch the scene unfold from the vantage point of the Café Glacier, which has a panoramic view of both the square and the Koutoubia mosque, the other dominant feature in the centre of the medina.

If you want to escape the bustle entirely, you can find solace in one of Marrakech's *riads* – traditional homes centred around a courtyard – many of which have been converted into stylish boutique hotels in recent years. They are typically hidden behind sturdy, thick, wooden doors, and there is no way of knowing that these conceal retreats with interiors that make you feel you are in an art gallery. Rooms are arranged around the courtyard, so all the windows face inwards overlooking this cool inner sanctum. Stepping into a *riad* is to step into a haven removed from the chaos, noise and hustle of the city, where you can unwind, relax and rest before your next shopping spree.

Souk mosque door

Ornate ceiling and lantern, Dar Les Cigognes

ⓘ ....

Several airlines, including Royal Air Maroc, fly daily to Marrakech. Across from the
Royal Palace and the Badi Palace, Dar Les Cigognes is one of Marrakech's luxurious *riads*. A merchant's house in the 17th century, it has been carefully restored
and the rooms individually decorated. They include the lavish Sahara room with
a desert landscape mural, and the Harem room with its red and gold furnishings.
Dar Les Cigognes gets its name from the storks that nest on its ramparts (*dar* is
Arab for 'house' and *cigognes* is French for 'storks'). Local guides are available
to help visitors find their way around the complex alleyways of the souk.

Post box and leather foot stool in the souk

Following thousands of wildebeest travelling en masse across the great plains of the Serengeti provides an awesome opportunity to witness one of the last great animal migrations on the planet. Nowhere else can you see such concentrations not only of wildebeest, but also of zebra and Thomson's gazelle, which join the 1450-km migration. An estimated 1.8 million wildebeest, constantly on the move, flood into the Serengeti in a never-ending quest for good grazing.

Wildebeest running to find water

Set on a high interior plateau, the Serengeti National Park was established in 1951, and 30 years later became a UNESCO World Heritage Site and Biosphere Reserve. Covering almost 15,000 sq. km, it is the first and largest of Tanzania's national parks. Along with the migration, you can see a massive variety of animals, including the safari 'big five' – lion, elephant, buffalo, leopard and rhino – which all live in the Serengeti.

On board a four-wheel-drive safari vehicle, specially adapted for spotting game, you can safely follow the epic journey. Local knowledge

Following wildebeest
The Serengeti, Tanzania

Zebra shelter under an isolated tree on the Serengeti's grass plains

Lions often seek shade during the midday heat

Giraffe wander the open plains

and communication between guides and drivers is very good, and the animals' daily movements are closely monitored, which maximizes the likelihood that the migration will be tracked and found. When it is spotted, the drama can keep you captivated for hours.

Running and trotting through the golden, waist-high grasses, the massed ranks of wildebeest create a hazy smokescreen of dust as they kick and bound, their heads distinctively tossing and dipping, tails swishing back and forth. Males do battle, or rut, to establish their territory at the beginning of the migration, gathering as many females as possible with which to mate. As the migration moves on, small gangs of successful bulls can be seen herding groups of a couple of hundred females, the males' distinctive, low-pitched brays echoing above the clatter of thousands of hoofs.

The start of the migratory cycle varies every year and is entirely dependent on when the rains come. Generally, herds begin to move from the grass plains in the south in May as water supplies dry up, heading northwards to the woodlands. En route they pass along the

Grumeti River and through the Western Corridor before eventually arriving in Kenya's Masai Mara National Reserve in about June. Throughout this hazardous journey they face attack from predators like lions, hyenas, jackals and cheetahs. During the unavoidable, high-tension river crossings tens of thousands of wildebeest die when they are snatched by crocodiles, while many others simply drown in the frenzy. The equally risky return journey starts again in November, to get the females back to the nutritious, southern grasslands to calve.

Other players on the great safari stage of the Serengeti include bulky water buffalos with intimidating horns and distinctly moody and not-to-be-messed-with stares. Herds of giraffes can be spotted wandering the open plains, stretching their long necks upwards to trim the acacia trees, while families of playful baboons tumble and

Wildebeest

Zebra often stand nose to tail to increase awareness of attack

Elephants disturb a vulture

mock fight at their feet. Famous also for its lions, the Serengeti is one of the best places to get close to the untamed force of these big cats. You may see a pride of them lazing in the sun or feeding after a kill. At night you might even hear a lone male roaring around your camp. And the show doesn't stop there. You could get sightings of elephants trampling through woodlands and trumpeting at anything in their way, hippos wallowing in muddy pools watched by stealthy crocs and an elusive leopard sneaking up a tree for shade.

Lion stretching under an acacia tree at dusk

Relaxing in a luxury tented camp

Afternoon safari drives are popular

As well as touring the park in a four-wheel-drive, another way to view the endless plains is to take to the skies in a hot-air balloon. Floating sedately through the air, with only the occasional thrust of the burner breaking the silence, you will enjoy the ultimate panoramic view. You may literally come back to earth with a bump as the wicker basket touches the ground, but you will probably be more concerned about what might just be watching you from behind the tall grasses.

ⓘ ··

Several airlines, including British Airways, fly to Dar es Salaam. Many tour operators run safaris in the Serengeti National Park to suit most budgets. Abercrombie & Kent organize luxury tented camp safaris that follow the migration. Safari life often involves getting up early for a game drive at dawn, and returning to the camp for breakfast. In the late afternoon the animals that have been resting in the shade during the midday heat, such as cheetah and lion, reappear.

The Rajput-built fort at Chittaurgarh covers over 279 hectares

Rajasthan is a region of maharajas' ornate palaces and hill-top forts, empty deserts and vibrant cities – and if you have only seven days to spare the best way to absorb what it has to offer is by boarding the exclusive Palace on Wheels train.

Situated in north-west India and bordered by Pakistan to the west, Gujarat to the south and the Punjab and Haryana to the north, Rajastahn is the home of the Rajputs, a ruling class who held power for over 1000 years until India's independence from Britain in 1947. They doggedly followed a code of chivalry like that of medieval European knights, and their bravery and sense of honour are

Woman entering Jaswant Thada in Jodhpur

legendary. They preferred to die rather than surrender to invaders, and once in the 14th century and twice in the 16th, when the city of Chittaurgarh was besieged, the women committed mass suicide (*jauhar*), throwing themselves on to pyres, and the men covered themselves with their ashes before riding out to face the enemy and annihilation.

When you first enter the Palace on Wheels at Delhi Cant station it is like stepping back in time to the era when maharajas rode the train. Elegantly attired *khidmatgers* (attendants) wearing deep-red turbans and silk waist sashes usher you in and whisk your bags away, before magically disappearing and then reappearing with cold drinks.

If this isn't enough to make you feel like royalty you will also be addressed as Maharaja or Maharanee.

Today's carriages are replicas rather than the original rolling stock, but the maharajas would recognize many of the materials and designs used in the furnishings. Inside each compartment crushed-velvet throws, embroidered in gold and red, cover the beds, and traditional Indian ink drawings, portraying court life, hang in the corridors and sitting room.

As the outskirts of Delhi slip out of view and are replaced by open countryside, with farmers working the fields, sacred cows wandering in the dust and village life chaotically spilling on to the trackside, you can find a comfortable seat in the bar and settle down with a gin and tonic. When you retire to bed the train keeps moving through the night, travelling south-west from Delhi to the first port of call: Jaipur, the hectic state capital where camels, cows and India's ubiquitous Ambassador cars vie for space in bustling streets.

When you enter the walled old city, the 'Pink City', you will have to be quick on your feet to dodge rickshaw drivers and traders touting their wares. The five-storey Palace of the Winds (Hawa Mahal) is one of the most ornate examples of the city's pink sandstone buildings. Close by, what looks like an open-air sculpture park is the Jantar Mantar observatory – a bizarre collection of gigantic devices that are still used for celestial calculations. The real highlight of a visit to Jaipur lies a short distance out of town at the Amber Fort perched on a high rocky bluff, which will give you your first glimpse into how the maharajas lived.

Travelling further westwards you enter the heart of the Thar Desert and come to the 'Golden City' of Jaisalmer. Thrusting upwards out of the barren landscape, the huge bulk of its imposing sandstone fortress, which glows golden in the sunset, has an almost otherworldly quality as it towers over the city below. Frequently

Peacock doorway at Jaipur palace

Ornate *havelies* (merchants' houses) at Jaisalmer

described as a gigantic sandcastle, its fortifications open into a labyrinth of streets and alleyways. Inside Jaisalmer you will see decorative *havelies*, the richly ornamental homes of Rajasthan merchants.

To experience life in the surrounding desolate plains, swap the Palace on Wheels for a 'ship of the desert' and explore the rolling sand dunes of Sam, just over 40 km from Jaisalmer, on a camel. The pitching roll of its gait, as you sit on a saddle straddling its hump, can take some getting used to.

To the east, colour strikes again in Jodhpur, home of the famous riding breeches. Known as the 'Blue City', it is punctuated with a patchwork of cornflower-blue front doors that denote the houses of the Brahmin priestly caste. The remarkable Meherangarh Fort sprawls above the city on the hillside.

Ranthambhor National Park provides a complete contrast to city sights. Its tigers are world-famous – it is considered the best place in

View of the city of Udaipur from Lake Palace Hotel

Glass mosaics at Lake Palace Hotel, Udaipur

Udaipur seen from the roof of Lake Palace Hotel

India for sighting these powerful cats – and you track them with a professional guide, on board a safari vehicle. Seeing a tiger's brown and black-striped coat dart from the surrounding undergrowth is an exciting moment.

Flashes of colour come in a different form the following day, in the vibrant ornamental gardens and on the cushioned roof balconies of the famous Lake Palace Hotel on Jag Niwas Island in Lake Pichola, in the romantic city of Udaipur, the 'Venice of the East'.

As the train heads back to Delhi there's still time to pull into Agra to see India's most romantic monument: the Taj Mahal. One of the wonders of the world, the beautiful, white marble Mogul mausoleum was built by the heartbroken Emperor Shah Jahan as a symbol of his unending love for his wife, who died in childbirth.

While there are many ways to get around Rajasthan, when it comes to immersing yourself in its history-rich culture none is better than travelling in your own mobile palace.

ⓘ ··

It is possible to book the Palace on Wheels via several tour companies, including Trans Indus, a specialist Asia operator. The train often gets booked up months ahead, so reserve your place early. Although the full journey lasts one week, it is possible to do any of the individual sections en route, so you can choose to stay on board for one night or more. Many of the sights involve some walking, so try to avoid the hottest time of year (April to June) when temperatures can reach 45°C.

Lake Palace Hotel, Udaipur

Trekking Torres del Paine
Patagonia, Chile

The striking spires, or Torres, that give their name to the park

Grazing the sky with their ragged, saw-toothed summits, the red granite peaks of the Torres del Paine national park are the popular icons of Patagonia, one of the wildest places on the planet. Remote, unpredictable and committing, the park has a network of trekking trails that are hard to rival. They encompass a clutch of iceberg-strewn, azure and jade lakes, white-water rivers and waterfalls, and the largest glaciers in the southern hemisphere outside Antarctica. It is unsurprising, then, that Torres del Paine is often dubbed the world's most spectacular national park.

Covering some 240,000 hectares, this UNESCO Biosphere Reserve is usually approached by bus or ferry via the small town of Puerto Natales. Some 500 km south of Puerto Montt, the gateway to Chilean Patagonia, Natales is set on the shores of the dramatic Last Hope Sound (Seno Ultima Esperanza). From otherworldly cloud formations

and menacing storms to unbelievable sunsets, this vast body of windswept waters can be a show in itself.

If you have time, the best way to reach Puerto Natales is by taking the ferry from Puerto Montt. It threads its way along the route of Charles Darwin's *Beagle*, through the hundreds of islands that line the Chilean south-west coastline, where icebergs and whales are common

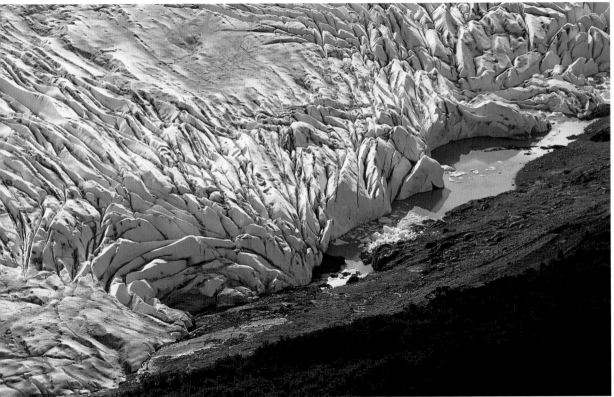

Fissured surface of Glacier Grey

sights. The four-day journey is a fantastic introduction to Patagonia, and, compared to almost any other cruise, an absolute bargain.

From Natales a four-hour bus ride along 112 km of dirt roads to the park entrance gives you plenty of time to contemplate the meaning of 'remote' as you drive through uninhabited countryside. Once inside Torres del Paine, the more serious trekkers take off on the Paine Circuit, a six- to eight-day epic – but navigationally straight-forward – route that is well worth getting fit for. While the other trails, such as the not-to-be-missed trek to the soaring pinnacles (Torres) that give their name to the park, are magnificent the circuit is undoubtedly the one to attempt, given the time and ability. You can tag the one- to two-day Torres trail on to the start or end of it. If it is

Glacier Grey forms part of the great southern Patagonia ice field

solitude you are after, avoid embarking on the circuit for a day or two after the ferry pulls into Puerto Natales, bringing with it a cargo of eager hikers.

Weather permitting (snow sometimes closes the highest pass), the 100-km circuit takes you around, through and over the Paine massif. It is best tackled anticlockwise – in this direction the scenery

Trekkers can cross Lago Grey by boat for views of the Paine massif

Looking down over Glacier Grey

improves constantly and the trail builds to the tougher sections. En route, you encounter lush meadows, cross small rivers and skirt beautiful wilderness lakes like Lago Dickson, surrounded by ice-topped mountains. Other lakes, such as Laguna Siete Perros (Seven Dogs), brim with icebergs and provide a stark contrast to the dense forests that line the lower to mid levels of the massif.

There are several challenging climbs to high passes, some of which have steep descents that offer little respite for weary legs, but the scenery is always spellbinding. Any aches and pains are forgotten when you look down at the immense, fissured valley of ice that is Glacier Grey. This remnant of the great southern Patagonian icefield, which once encased the entire region, is about 1500 years old and regularly calves chunks of ice into Lago Grey, the home run on the circuit.

For those in search of a touch of luxury, Hosteria Grey on the shores of Lago Grey is an outstanding if somewhat ungainly lodge, where the wind is kept at bay by double glazing and normal hotel service is resumed. Though we wouldn't recommend that you spend your entire time there, it is an ideal end-of-trek treat. Experience the alluring wilderness that is Torres del Paine just once, and it will always call you back.

(i) ···

Trekking the Paine Circuit involves either sleeping in huts, which must be booked ahead, or camping. You will also need to reserve accommodation at the Hosteria Grey well in advance. The best, but also the busiest, time to go to Torres del Paine is from December to March. Blue Green Adventures run a full range of adventure trips, including trekking, biking and horse trekking. Venture south of Patagonia and it's 'next stop Antarctica', so expect – and equip yourself for – some wild weather during the trek. It may not arrive, but if it does being caught out will be a recipe for misery. The winds, in particular, can be ferocious.

Exploring around Lago Dickson

Sunset paddle to the islets at Candelero, Espíritu Santo

With cactus-studded desert mountains plunging into tranquil turquoise bays, gliding manta rays and pods of migrating orcas, the uninhabited island of Espíritu Santo is one of the world's best spots for sea-kayaking. Just under 32 km long, Espíritu Santo is joined at low tide by a narrow isthmus to its northern neighbour, Isla Partida. The islands shelter in the shimmering Sea of Cortes, which separates mainland Mexico and the finger-like Baja peninsula. With warm water, and sunshine pretty well guaranteed from October to May, you won't mind getting wet as you learn the kayak-capsize drill.

Sea-Kayaking Baja
Espíritu Santo, Mexico

Kayaks at dawn on Espíritu Santo

Only 29 km north of the coastal town of La Paz, volcanic Espíritu Santo split from the mainland seven million years ago, after a devastating earthquake along the San Andreas fault. While it is a land-bridge island, connected to the mainland under water, it feels like a peaceful wilderness that could be miles from anywhere.

Paddling past multicoloured volcanic rock near Candelero

A trip to Espíritu Santo starts with a boat journey aboard the 'mother ship', a motorized skiff, on to which kayaks, provisions and equipment are loaded. If you opt for a fully catered trip most of this stays on board, and you won't have to carry a tent or food when you kayak.

A popular place to begin kayaking is at Los Islotes, two rocky islets to the north of Isla Partida, which are dusted in what the local guides euphemistically describe as 'Mexican snow' – the pungent droppings of the resident squawking birds. However, it's the islets' 300-strong colony of Californian sea lions, and the chance of coming face to face with one when you snorkel amongst them, that is really interesting.

Cacti are found across the entire island

A refreshing soak on Espíritu Santo

Espíritu Santo may not be inhabited by people but it is teeming with life both above and below the crystal-clear water. Peer over the side of your kayak to spot over 500 different species of colourful tropical fish, like the bull's eye pufferfish with its big lips and patchy stripes, and the king angel fish with its angular, yellow tail and iridescent blue body, and you may want to drop anchor, pull on a snorkel mask and fins, and dive out of your kayak.

Cacti at sunrise on Espíritu Santo

Bay overlooked by Pericue Indian cave

With a little luck you may have a close encounter with some of the sea's larger animals – one-third of the world's whales and dolphins live in the Sea of Cortes. From January to March is best for spotting migrating grey whales and humpbacks, while April and May are good times for seeing blue, sperm and fin whales. More likely sightings at any time of year are colonies of breeding sea lions or the odd sea turtle. In the skies above, seabirds like the frigate bird, with its forked tail, glide, swoop and soar. Even more eye-catching for kayakers are Californian brown pelicans diving for food. When they are not fishing they frequently stand sentinel on rocks.

A real treat lies in store at Candelero, further south on the western side of Espíritu Santo, where you camp. The most attractive beach on the island, it is backed by red, rock cliffs. A jagged ridge divides the bay and a rocky finger crowned with cardón cactus leads into the water. Three small islets, which in themselves make for an interesting, short paddle trip, lead away to the horizon and form striking silhouettes at sunset.

If you continue paddling down this coast towards Playa Ballena, a climb up the steep sides of a bay will take you to a 5000-year-old cave that was used as a shelter by Pericue Indians, the semi-nomadic tribe that once lived on Espíritu Santo. They roamed the island, dived for clams and scallops, and used sharpened sticks to snare fish.

Whether it's the wild silence of a starlit deserted beach or the serene glow of dusk on the gently lapping sea, you will enjoy experiences that you hardly thought possible when you sea-kayak around Espíritu Santo. All that's required is a bit of paddle power.

ⓘ ···

Baja Outdoor Activities provides a variety of trips to Espíritu Santo. These include nine-day circumnavigations of the island and 'Quick Escapes' that last four days and three nights. On fully catered trips food is provided and equipment is carried on a support boat. There is also a cooperative catering option whereby everyone mucks in and carries their own equipment. Both include experienced and qualified guides.

Kayaking by red volcanic rock

Paddling toward Playa Ballena

Rice-boat cruising
Kerala, India

Idly cruising down Kerala's backwater canals in a luxuriously converted rice boat, past swathes of palm trees, vast paddy fields and small villages, has to be the most relaxing way to discover this unique part of India.

A *kettuvallam* rice boat at sunset

A lush green, vibrant finger of land bordering the Arabian Sea, the state of Kerala stretches for 550 km along India's south-west coast. Nestling behind a strip of idyllic beaches and sandy bays are the famous backwaters, an intricate network of canals, lagoons and lakes that take you into the heart of the country's 'rice bowl'.

According to legend the state was created by Parasurama, the sixth incarnation of the god Vishnu, who wanted a virgin land in which to perform yoga. He threw an axe into the sea and the area of water covered by his throw retreated and formed this labyrinth of waterways. Aboard a *kettuvallam*, the Keralan longboat once used to transport rice from the surrounding fields, you can slip through a landscape that has barely changed over the centuries. Children splash in the shallows, women wash clothes and fieldworkers cultivate the same lush lands as their forefathers. Everywhere you are greeted by smiling faces.

Cochin is known for its Chinese fishing nets, seen here at sunset

Narrow canalways, backed with thick dense trees, take you to the open vistas of Vembanad, the biggest freshwater lake in India. Plantations where cocoa, coconuts and mangoes are grown sit alongside small mud-brick villages, churches, mosques and colourful Hindu temples. Here and there even narrower channels, wide enough only for dugout canoes, branch off and lead further into this intricate maze.

Traditional fishing near Kainady Homestay

On your *kettuvallam* you can laze on the raised, cushioned deck at the front of the boat – a perfect viewing platform. Further back, a curved, palm-plaited roof provides a shady covering that leads to the bedroom and kitchen areas. As you navigate the serene waterways, the delicious smell of fresh fish seasoned with a blend of local spices, cooked by your crew, is probably the only thing that will stir you into activity.

The popular backwater area, known as the Kuttanad, extends for 75 km from Kollam in the south to Cochin in the north. Also known as Kochi, Cochin is where you will begin to get a feel for the vibrancy of Kerala, a region that has attracted visitors in search of spices and sandalwood for the last 2000 years.

Its coast was known to the Phoenicians and Romans, and later the Arabs and Chinese, long before it was 'discovered' by Vasco da Gama in 1498. These diverse influences are still reflected in the sights and sounds of the city. Take a stroll on the northern shore of Fort Cochin (the old part of the city) in the early morning and you will see ancient Chinese nets being lowered and raised by teams of local fishermen searching the bountiful waters for a catch. In the evening catch a performance of Kathakali – an art form unique to the state, it combines dance, story-telling and mime. Alternatively, relax by experiencing an Ayurvedic treatment, a holistic medical system that is found across India but is particularly dominant in Kerala.

Fresh tomatoes at Cochin market

A converted *kettuvallam* rice boat for cruising the backwaters

Cochin's Chinese fishing nets are cantilevered with large boulders

Early morning sees the arrival of fresh fish at Fort Cochin's shoreline

If you have time for yet one more contrast, it is worth travelling from the warm backwaters to the cool hill station of Munnar and its surrounding tea plantations. About 130 km east of Cochin, the area is the tea-growing hub of Kerala. A blanket of rich green covers mountain slopes where workers pick the leaves by hand.

Whether you are enjoying the fresh air of the mountains or slipping through Kerala's waterways, the pace of life slows right down in this verdant, laid-back part of India.

Fisherman climbing a Chinese net

ⓘ ··

Among other tour companies, Trans Indus, a specialist operator, organizes tailor-made tours that allow you to explore Kerala fully, including cruising the backwaters on a rice boat and staying on a tea plantation. The Windermere Estate offers bungalow accommodation in the heart of a working plantation. At the Kainady Heritage Homestay you can stay in a traditional homestead and experience family life on the backwaters. Situated near the towns of Kottayam and Alappuzha on the Manimala River, you can explore the backwaters further by boat or canoe, or go fishing or bird-watching, as well as visiting temples and churches.

Skiing the Vallée Blanche
Chamonix, France

Hidden among the high mountains of the French Alps, above Chamonix, the Vallée Blanche is Europe's longest off-piste ski run, and gives unique access to a wild snow-swept, ice-carved landscape. For intermediate skiers, remote towering Alpine peaks, including Mont Blanc, crevasse-strewn glaciers like the Mer de Glace (Sea of Ice), and limitless powder snow await. Quite unlike any run anywhere else in the world, it provides a skiing experience that will take you to entirely new heights.

Down in Chamonix it may be hard to imagine even penetrating the imposing mountain range that rises high above, let alone skiing 22 km through it. From the valley floor, at 1100 metres, the peaks can

Skiing on the Glacier du Géant

Exiting the ice tunnel on Aiguille du Midi

seem a very long way away. However, the world's highest cable car transports you effortlessly door to door.

If you have a head for heights this experience alone is not to be missed, even if you have no intention to ski on. From the second lift-station you take the longest single-span cable-car journey in the world, climbing up and over what looks like an impossibly sheer, blunt rock-face. In a little over five minutes you are in rarefied air at 3802 metres, on the north peak of the Aiguille du Midi. Take the lift to the viewing platform at 3842 metres for your first glimpse of what is to come. Ski tracks weave off into the sublime, snow-filled valley, which is backdropped by a panorama of classic mountaineering

peaks like Grandes Jorasses, and the distant Matterhorn on the Italian–Swiss border.

Getting from this high point to the start of the ski run is what makes you begin to realize that this is not like any normal day on the piste. Expert guides usher clients into orderly lines, fasten climbing harnesses on them and then carefully clip them into a safety-rope system. Stepping out through an ice tunnel brings you on to a knife-edge arête, a ridge that you must pick your way down. The path follows this at a 30-degree angle, with fixed ropes on either side for handrails. It's not as treacherous as it might look but, with a 2700-metre drop to Chamonix on one side and a 50-degree slope on the other, traversing it can understandably seem fairly hair-raising when you're wearing a pair of ski boots.

Looking down over Glacier du Géant

Skiers on Glacier du Géant

Easy ski terrain near the bottom of the Vallée Blanche

Once you're down take the most popular route, the Vrai (Classic) Vallée Blanche and gently weave through the Glacier du Géant. This first downhill sweep comes to an end at the Sérac du Géant, a glacial area of broken blocks of ice, crevasses and ice caves. Here the run narrows and, like finding a path through a maze, you must pick a way through a strange, frozen landscape. The services of a guide and a cool head will ensure safe passage. This world of blue and turquoise ice eventually leads you to the Refuge du Requin at 2516 metres – the 'Shark's Refuge', named after the protruding fin-shaped mountain behind the restaurant hut.

Beneath the hut, an ice-strewn serac field has to be negotiated to reach the intriguingly named Salle à Manger (Dining Room). This broad area above the Glacier du Tacul earned its name because it offers the perfect picnic spot beneath the mighty peak of Grandes Jorasses. For the unwary skier or snowboarder it can be a minefield where deep crevasses can also make a meal of you.

The crevasse field above the Salle à Manger

Skiing below the Aiguille du Midi

    The Mer de Glace, a huge creeping body of ice about 240 metres thick and the second-largest glacier in the Alps, stretches a further 7 km, sloping gently down towards Montenvers. After a steady descent you climb a steepish set of steps past ice caves to a cable car that links you to a scenic mountain railway. The gentle ride back to Chamonix will give you ample time to realize that, after tackling the world's greatest off-piste run, skiing on-piste will never be the same again.

ⓘ ....

Hiring a qualified mountain guide is recommended unless you are an experienced off-piste skier. He or she will provide specialist safety equipment like avalanche transceivers and climbing harnesses. There are many options for organizing skiing at Chamonix. Specialist ski operator Neilson offer packages that include accommodation in their traditional Red Mountain Lodge Chalet in the heart of Chamonix and tailor-made descents through the Vallée Blanche.

Traversing to find fresh powder snow

Cycling among rice paddies
Hanoi to Saigon, Vietnam

An abundant land of endless rice paddies and fertile highland ranges, with a beguiling South China Sea coastline, Vietnam offers the best and most varied cycling to be found anywhere in South-east Asia. Add its fascinating Communist history under the leadership of national hero Ho Chi Minh, or Uncle Ho as he is affectionately known by the Vietnamese, and the route from Hanoi to Saigon makes for the ride of a lifetime.

Everywhere you pedal you will be greeted by smiling Vietnamese faces, waving hands and shouted hellos. Nothing seems to give the local cyclists more pleasure than having you ride alongside them for a while; and nothing is more memorable than seeing them beaming at you from beneath their trademark conical straw hats. This is cycling at its most sublime.

Planting rice near Nha Trang

Rice workers planting patchwork paddies along the road to Nha Trang

Vietnamese cyclist on the road to Hué

Riding all the way from Hanoi, the modern capital, to Saigon would take even a fit cyclist several weeks. The more appealing option is to travel with an operator who provides full bus support, which allows you to cycle the best parts of the journey and still make it to Saigon within two weeks. A popular starting point for riding is the old imperial city of Hué, a 13-hour train trip south from Hanoi.

The country's capital during the Nguyen Dynasty (1802–1945), Hué retains many of its original palaces and pagodas. Negotiating the countless motorbikes and cycles that throng its roads and swarm around you at traffic lights can be slightly unnerving at first, but once you go with the flow you'll be able to relax and enjoy a human-powered spectacle to marvel at. Your first stopover, the tomb of the emperor Tu Duc, who reigned from 1847 to 1883, is a 30-minute ride

Hoi An market

away on the outskirts of the city, set in tranquil woodland on the edge of lotus-flower-filled Luu Khiem Lake.

Highway 1 takes you south from Hué, and is lined with rice paddies in endless shades of green, where workers in conical hats bend gracefully to push rice plants rhythmically into the flooded earth. The next cycling stopover is the ancient port of Hoi An, where centuries of foreign trading have left a captivating mix of cultures and influences, from Japanese and Chinese to French and Dutch. A stroll along Tran Phu Street takes you past colourfully decorated Chinese assembly halls, merchant houses and tiny shops with mossy-tiled roofs where you can buy wood crafts, paper lanterns and silk.

No visit to Vietnam is possible without being made aware of the impact of the 1965–75 Vietnam War (the American War, as it is known by

Market stall at Dalat, the country's major vegetable-growing region

Flooded rice paddies on the road to Nha Trang

the Vietnamese). A 24-km detour on the journey south towards Quang Ngai takes you through rice paddies to Son My village – scene of the war's most infamous massacre, often referred to as the My Lai incident, when American soldiers killed 504 villagers. Its memorial park has an exhibition of chilling photographs taken on the day of the attack.

From Quang Ngai the best way is up, and Highway 19 poses a stiff cycling challenge as it climbs steeply over the An Khe Pass into the Truong Son mountain range and takes you on to the highland centres of Play Ku and Buon Ma Thuot. On the plateau the landscape changes from rice paddies to extensive coffee and tea plantations, and small family plots that grow just about any vegetable and flower you care to name. Life is simpler here and the rolling road makes for a welcome, if more energetic, break from cycling along the coastal flatlands.

Next comes a breathtaking ride along a winding road that eventually plunges down to Nha Trang on the coast. This is the unabashed coastal resort of Vietnam, with a boulevard and beach that wouldn't look out of place in the USA, but it hasn't lost its charm. It

Children near An Khe Pass

Cyclists carry huge loads, even on the busy streets of Saigon

Women transporting firewood through Hoi An

Traditional coracle fishing boats offshore from Nha Trang

Rowing to market

has several impressive temples that date back to the Champa civilization that flourished on the central Vietnam coast from 200 to 1720. Before heading for Saigon, a final climb into the highlands takes you to the former French hill station of Dalat. Be warned: the road to get there is dauntingly steep and long, so the support bus is the best option once you have cycled 100 km or so along the flats from Nha Trang to the Dalat turn-off at Phan Rang.

The jewel at the end of the ride is Saigon, one of South-east Asia's most dynamic cities. Officially renamed Ho Chi Minh City in 1975, it is chaotic, industrious, cultured and stylish – the perfect place to find a bar and celebrate your cycling exploits.

ⓘ ··

The monsoon season is best avoided unless you like cycling in a poncho, so aim to travel in Vietnam between late November and March. World Expeditions offer an excellent, fully supported two-week cycling tour from Hanoi to Saigon, with very good hotel accommodation and English-speaking local guides to ease your way. Vietnamese food, especially the seafood, is outstanding. There are international airports at both Hanoi and Saigon. When you are in Saigon a visit to the Cu Chi tunnels, where the Viet Cong lived and hid during the Vietnam War, is a must-do.

Festival of the Sahara
Douz, Tunisia

When fiercely proud Bedouin nomads and their camel caravans converge on the Tunisian oasis town of Douz for the spectacular Festival of the Sahara, sand and sparks are bound to fly. The event is still relatively unknown outside Tunisia, but with camel racing, poetry competitions, tribal plays and traditional music, this flamboyant gathering is the best desert festival for your diary.

Mehari camels race to the finish line

Young Bedouin horse rider

Douz itself seems to float between the shimmering, endless dunes of the Great Eastern Erg and the mirage-making, ocean-sized salt flat of Chott El Jerid, in central Tunisia. Driving across the latter's 50-km-wide, blinding white expanse invokes thoughts of Antarctica, and is a sure-fire way to exhaust your supply of superlatives before you even reach the oasis.

The town is the social and trading hub for five Bedouin groups, with the 15,000-strong Mrazrig tribe holding sway. During spring, many tribesmen still move their sheep and goats south towards Ksar Ghilane to graze on the Nefazaoua plains. In winter they return to Douz to work on the date harvest, and it was this seasonal regrouping that first inspired the festival (nobody really knows when it started

Tribal musicians come from all over Tunisia

although it has been official for over 35 years). It was a chance for tribes to test each other's wits in games and horsemanship, a time for musical and poetical celebration, and an opportunity for youngsters to marry – a tradition that continues today.

Life for the Bedouin has always been a delicate balancing act between desert survival and oasis exuberance, a relationship mirrored in the location of H'Niche Stadium, a one-stand, open-sided affair that is site of the main action. Built on the very edge of town, it is held in place on one side by overhanging palm trees and dissolves seamlessly into wind-whipped dunes on the other.

With crowds filling the whole stadium, the festival bursts into life with the thud of drums and the piercing tones of the flute-like *zoukara*. The players, swathed in billowing white skirts and bright red waistcoats, their fezzes topped with lengthy black tassels, whirl like

Tribal elders parade at the festival opening

Drums and *zoukaras* set the festival rhythm

spinning tops, almost drilling themselves into the ground. Line after line of Bedouin tribesmen fire ear-cracking shotgun volleys into the sand as horse riders behind them fight to control their fiery mounts.

The most prestigious event is the camel race. With around £2000 at stake, victory must be won at any cost. In a loping version of the Olympic 800 metres, the pale-cream mehari camels – speedy sprinters normally employed to search out new pastures ahead of caravans – race shoulder to shoulder. After a series of qualifying

Dancers twirl during the festival opening parade

heats, the final is on the fourth and last day, and includes two exhausting laps of the circuit. Such is the prize, it is not unknown for fights to break out between the jockeys.

In between the sporting action, an elaborate, traditional play unfolds with the Saharan dunes as a stage. It tells the story of a brave Bedouin warrior, Mandour, who falls in love with a girl from a rival tribe. Trouble and strife follow before... well, let's not spoil the ending. Another event well worth catching is the unique 'hair dance'. Dozens of girls, clothed in vivid dresses and with their faces veiled, kneel on the ground and swing their long hair around in great swishing arcs to the sound of hypnotic music, until they collapse.

As well as the final of the camel race, the fourth day also sees Sloughi greyhound racing, and a sand-hockey competition with the teams using shepherd's crooks for hockey sticks. However, the most spectacular display is by acrobatic horsemen who, at full gallop, bounce around and on and off their mounts, like vaulting gymnasts. A rousing procession formally closes the festival and within hours the site is cleared. Black woollen tents are dismantled, earthenware cooking pots packed and camel trains prepared.

As the Bedouin meander through an ocean of sandy waves towards the targetless horizon, it seems that their journey home will take for ever. There is no doubt that their collective body-clock will bring them back next year, but their speedy departure suggests that their hearts belong more to the Sahara than the oasis.

ⓘ ....

The festival is held at the end of November or the beginning of December; the actual date is different every year. Douz is packed during the festivities, so book your accommodation early. Other events, including a 'Miss Sahara' competition, take place in the town in the evenings. The first day and the last day of the festival are usually the most spectacular and boisterous.

Bedouin horsemanship is a star attraction

Tallinn and St Olav's Church from Toompea Hill

Set like a fairy-tale city on the Estonian shores of the Baltic Sea, Tallinn is at the forefront of the resurgence being enjoyed by the former Soviet Baltic States as they explore and celebrate their independence from the USSR. Northern Europe's oldest capital, this colourful city is largely unspoilt by modern development, and exploring it on foot or by bike is an unforgettable journey through the Middle Ages.

Estonia broke free of Soviet domination in August 1991. Just 13 years later, in May 2004, it was accepted into the European Union, completing its transition to a strong, independent state. It hasn't looked back since. Vibrant and exciting, Tallinn embodies this new era and there is no better place to taste Estonians' fierce pride in their country than in the supremely preserved, medieval Old Town at the heart of the city.

Buildings with turrets and red-tiled roofs line the twist of cobbled alleyways in this UNESCO World Heritage Site, which is protected by remarkably intact fortress walls and watchtowers. Thanks largely to these defences – 26 of the towers still survive – the city suffered little

Market stalls in Town Hall Square

Tallinn's Old Town is full of red tiled roofs

damage throughout its history and boasts a string of original houses, state buildings and medieval churches. The towering, Gothic St Olav's Church was once the tallest building in northern Europe, at 159 metres high, and its distinctive green spire still dominates the city today.

Shopping in Tallinn centres on Town Hall Square, where fairs, political meetings and even executions used to be the principal attractions. These days, you can bargain-hunt at its traditional wooden stalls or sit in any of a number of fashionable, lively cafés that line its perimeter and watch young Estonians showing off their latest designer clothes. During the summer, medieval life returns to the square with the exuberant Old Town Days carnival. And don't miss out on a visit to the impressive Town Hall itself, which dates back to the very start of the 13th century.

For a different perspective on the Old Town and Tallinn's location on the Baltic Sea, wind your way up through the fortress walls to Toompea Hill, which overlooks the city and boasts the imposing and ornate Alexander Nevsky Cathedral. Built in 1900 by Nicholas II,

Russia's last tsar, the multidomed building glitters with gold mosaics. If you wait around, you'll find yourself resounding to the 11 booming bells in its central towers that herald the start of a service. Further along the hill, several lookout points provide stunning views over the city and its rooftops to the Baltic.

On the way down to the lower part of the Old Town, the path detours around the massive Kiek in de Kök cannon tower. With a circumference of 17 metres, and walls so thick it would probably take a hundred years to demolish them, it retains a sense of impenetrable defiance. Another tower worth stopping off at is the Maiden Tower, where prostitutes were once imprisoned. One of the city's most unusual houses dates from the 14th century and belonged to the Brotherhood of Black Heads, a powerful group of merchants. Its green and red door is decorated with ornate carvings of golden flowers.

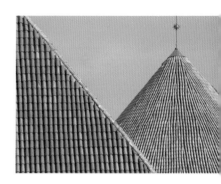

Turrets on the Old Town wall

Tallinn's Old Town from Toopea Hill

243

Tallinn's colourful Post Office

Cafés in Town Hall Square

No visit to Tallinn would be complete without a trip to the Baltic coastline, which will also give you a chance to see monuments of the Soviet era and the Second World War. The best way to get there is on a bicycle. Apart from Toompea Hill, the city and its surroundings are flat, so cycling doesn't require much effort. It's easy to hire a bike independently, but if you team up with a City Bike guide you will be able to avoid main roads and cycle through Tallinn's spacious parks and past palaces, like Kadriorg Palace, that belonged to the tsars. And when you reach the coast and look out over the blue, tranquil waters of the Baltic Sea, you may well sense the indefatigable and defiant spirit of the Estonians lapping in on the tide.

ⓘ

Several airlines fly to Tallinn. Estonia Air offer very good fares from many of Europe's major cities, which has sharply increased the number of people travelling there, even for weekend breaks. To make your stay in the city even more of a treat, book into one of several boutique hotels, such as the Three Sisters Hotel, which have been converted from merchants' houses. City Bike operate in the summer, and offer straightforward bike hire or a selection of guided rides.

Searching for pearls
Tahiti, French Polynesia

The search for a perfect black pearl, the highly prized jewel of French Polynesia, is a journey into the crystal-water paradise where the infamous HMS *Bounty* dropped anchor. Here its crew discovered palm-fringed beaches, a perpetually warm climate and exotic food, and mutinied when they were forced to leave. Today little has changed – but visitors can now acquire their own island treasure.

Tahiti's most important export, black pearls are cultured, rather than forming naturally, and take more than five years to grow. Although they are described as black, seen close up they are in fact iridescent, with peacock hues of green and purple. It is this variety in their colouring that makes them unique and such a sought-after prize.

Snorkelling from over-water bungalows on Manihi

Black pearl in its oyster shell at Tahaa

Searching for the perfect pearl – no two are the same – can take you to 35 different islands and 83 atolls, set amidst the vast, blue waters of the South Pacific.

Unspoilt Manihi, part of the Tuamotu Archipelago and a two-hour flight north-east of Tahiti, is just one of the island retreats you can head to. An island chain around a 60-km-long and 30-km-wide lagoon, it is every bit the white-sand, palm-lined paradise you might dream of, an ideal place to start your search. It also claims to be the original home of the world-famous black pearl – it was here that the first farm to cultivate the black-lipped oysters unique to French Polynesia went into operation, in 1965. Today Manihi is known as the 'black pearl paradise'.

Over-water bungalow at Manihi

Part of the joy of the search is that it involves so much more than a simple trip to a high street jeweller. Getting to grips with how the pearls come into existence, and finding out about the processes involved, offers a journey into a culture carved by the sea. Doing justice to the experience requires some exploration, and just getting to some of the 'black pearl' islands on small planes and boats presents a fresh adventure each time.

Manihi is no exception. From the air its islands look almost like a delicate pearl necklace on a cushion of deep-blue velvet. As the descent starts and the land takes shape you can begin to make out small clusters of over-water bungalows nestled on the inner lagoon – the perfect place to relax while you are on the atoll.

Arriving on Manihi will be one of your less conventional travelling experiences. The airport buildings were washed away by a cyclone in 1996, and there is nothing at the airstrip bar a small, wooden shelter with a palm-fringed roof to shade passengers waiting for their flight. You will be bedecked with a garland, given a seat on a golf buggy and chauffeured to your accommodation through a lane lined with coconut trees. Even better there is no baggage carousel.

Manihi has French Polynesia's biggest concentration of pearl farms – there are more than 60, dedicated to the painstaking and time-consuming process of cultivating the best possible pearls. A tour of a farm allows you to see how much goes into growing just one of them. A 'nucleus' is inserted into the pearl sac of an oyster and a piece of muscle from the black lips of another oyster is grafted on to it. This muscle grows around the nucleus and becomes a pearl. The graft, a lengthy process, is not always successful. Farmers expect that only 30 per cent of oysters will produce pearls, and that only 10 per cent of these will be of a high enough standard to sell. From a batch of 25,000 oysters only 3 per cent will be perfectly round, adding significantly to their value.

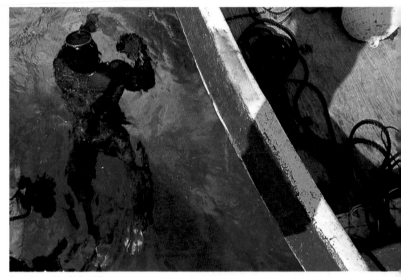

Pearl diver at Manihi Pearl Farm

If you want your search to be even more adventurous, head north-west of Tahiti to the lush green island of Tahaa, otherwise known as the 'Vanilla Island'. Here you can take to the water and tour the nearby farms aboard a traditional pirogue-style canoe. These boats are commonplace in French Polynesia, and are even used for room service in resorts, delivering breakfast direct to the doors of over-water bungalows.

The temptation to buy in such a beautiful, natural environment may prove to be irresistible – making your search for pearls more expensive than expected.

Frangipane flower at Tahaa

ⓘ ···

Exploring the French Polynesian islands is most easily done by plane. However, the aircraft are small and baggage weights need to be kept down, so it is advisable to pack light in order to avoid problems. Prices for food and drink tend to be quite high, especially on the outer islands where everything has to be flown in. Air New Zealand flies to Papeete on Tahiti via their Coral Route from Los Angeles. They provide daily connections from London to Los Angeles.

1 KLOCKA, SWEDEN

2 KAKADU, AUSTRALIA

3 ISTANBUL, TURKEY

4 CHAA CREEK, BELIZE

5 BORDEAUX, FRANCE

6 ZAMBEZI RIVER, ZAMBIA

7 SKELETON COAST, NAMIBIA

8 PRINCESS ROYAL ISLAND, CANADA

9 INVERLOCHY CASTLE, SCOTLAND

10 MOAB, USA

11 KHENTII, MONGOLIA

12 ANGEL FALLS, VENEZUELA

13 ANNAPURNA, NEPAL

14 VERONA, ITALY

15 BIG SUR, USA

16 GOLDEN CIRCLE, ICELAND

17 LAS VEGAS, USA

18 CHITWAN, NEPAL

19 GOLDEN, CANADA

20 ASWAN, EGYPT

21 PACAYA, GUATEMALA

22 FIORDLAND, NEW ZEALAND

23 WADI RUM, JORDAN

24 NEW ORLEANS, USA

25 DAHAB, EGYPT

26 PAKIRI BEACH, NEW ZEALAND

27 JINSHANLING, CHINA

28 PALEOCHORA, CRETE

29 DHONI MIGHILI, THE MALDIVES

30 MARRAKECH, MOROCCO

31 THE SERENGETI, TANZANIA

32 RAJASTHAN, INDIA

33 PATAGONIA, CHILE

34 ESPÍRITU SANTO, MEXICO

35 KERALA, INDIA

36 CHAMONIX, FRANCE

37 HANOI, VIETNAM

38 DOUZ, TUNISIA

39 TALLINN, ESTONIA

40 TAHITI, FRENCH POLYNESIA

There is a wealth of travel information available on the web, including general sites such as www.expedia.com, www. travelocity.com and www.travel.yahoo.com (Canadian travellers should visit www.expedia.ca, www.travelocity.ca and ca.travel.yahoo.com). You may also want to check government issued travel warnings by visiting www.travel.state.gov/travel warnings (Canadians should visit www.voyage.gc.ca/consular_home-en.asp).

Many countries require tourist visas, even for short stays, and you may need vaccinations, so contact a local travel agent as early as possible for specific information.

Airlines

Air China
www.airchina.com.cn/en

Air Canada
www.aircanada.com

Air Fiordland
www.airfiordland.com

Air Namibia
www.airnamibia.com.na

Air New Zealand
www.airnewzealand.com

Alitalia
www.alitalia.com

American Airlines
www.aa.com

British Airways
www.ba.com

Delta Airlines
www.delta.com

Egypt Air
www.egyptair.com.eg

Estonian Air
www.estonianair.com

Iceland Air
www.icelandair.com

Pacific Coastal Airlines
www.pacific-coastal.com

Qantas
www.qantas.com

Royal Air Maroc
www.royalairmaroc.com

Royal Jordanian Airlines
www.rja.com.jo

Scandinavian Airlines
www.scandinavian.net

Turkish Airlines
www.turkishairlines.com

United Airlines
www.united.com

Aboriginal dreaming, Australia

Tourism Australia
www.australia.com

Odyssey Safaris
www.odysaf.com.au

Camel trekking, Jordan

Desert Explorer
www.desertexplorer.net

Jordan Tourism Board
www.see-jordan.com

Châteaux and wine-tasting, France

Arblaster & Clarke
www.arblasterandclarke.com

French Tourist Office
www.francetourism.com

Climbing a volcano, Guatemala

Guatemala Tourist Commission
www.mayaspirit.com.gt

Crossing the divide, Turkey

Embassy of the Republic of Turkey, Washington, DC
www.turkishembassy.org

Ministry of Culture and Tourism
www.tourismturkey.org

Cycling among rice paddies, Vietnam

Vietnam National Administration of Tourism
www.vietnamtourism.com

World Expeditions
www.worldexpeditions.net

Discovering a medieval city, Estonia

Estonia Tourist Board
www.visitestonia.com

Three Sisters Hotel
www.threesistershotel.com

Discovering wild flowers, Crete

Explore Crete
www.explorecrete.com

Greek National Tourism Organization
www.gnto.gr

Dog-sledding, Sweden

Hotel Klocka Fjällgård
www.klockafjallgard.com

Swedish Travel & Tourism Council
www.visit-sweden.com

Driving Californian surf, USA

Big Sur Chamber of Commerce
www.bigsurcalifornia.org

California Travel and Tourism Commission
www.visitcalifornia.com

Exploring rainforest and reef, Belize

Abercrombie & Kent
www.abercrombiekent.com

Belize Tourism Board
www.belizetourism.org

Turtle Inn
www.turtleinn.com

Felucca down the Nile, Egypt

Experience Egypt
www.experience-egypt.com

Egyptian Tourist Authority
www.egypttourism.org

Festival of the Sahara, Tunisia

Tunisia National Tourist Office
www.tourismtunisia.com

Finding paradise, the Maldives

Dhoni Mighili
www.dhonimighili.com

Ministry of Tourism
www.visitmaldives.com.mv

Fly-fishing and whisky, Scotland

Inverlochy Castle
www.inverlochycastlehotel.com

Scottish Tourist Board
www.visitscotland.com

Flying safari, Namibia
Namibia Ministry of Environment
and Tourism
www.met.gov.na

Namibia Tourism Board
www.namibiatourism.com.na

Skeleton Coast Safaris
www.skeletoncoastsafaris.com

Wilderness Safaris
www.wilderness-safaris.com

Following wildebeest, Tanzania
Abercrombie & Kent
www.abercrombiekent.com

Tanzania Tourist Board
www.tanzaniatouristboard.com

Gambling and glitz, USA
Nevada Commission on Tourism
www.travelnevada.com

Heli-hiking in the Rockies, Canada
Canadian Helicopters
www.canadianhelicopters.com

Purcell Lodge
www.placeslesstravelled.com

Tourism British Columbia
www.hellobc.com

Hiking through arches, USA
Canyonlands National Park
www.nps.gov/cany

Slickrock Air Guides
www.slickrockairguides.com

Himalayan adventure, Nepal
Nepal Tourism Board
www.welcomenepal.com

Specialist Trekking
www.specialisttrekking.co.uk

**'Lost World' river journey,
Venezuela**
Angel Falls in Venezuela
www.salto-angel.com

Embassy of the Bolivian Republic of
Venezuela in the USA
www.embavenez-us.org

Palace on Wheels, India
Rajasthan Department of Tourism
www.rajasthantourism.gov.in

Palace on Wheels
www.palaceonwheels.net

Partying at Mardi Gras, USA
Mardi Gras
www.mardigras.com

New Orleans Convention and
Visitor Bureau
www.neworleanscvb.com

Pontchartrain Hotel
www.pontchartrainhotel.com

Red Sea diving, Egypt
Egyptian Tourism Network
www.tourism.egnet.net

Red Sea Virtual Dive Center
www.redseavdc.com

Rice-boat cruising, India
Department of Tourism
www.tourismofindia.com

Windermere Estate, Munnar
www.windermeremunnar.com

Riding elephants, Nepal
Nepal Home Page
www.nepalhomepage.com

Tourism Industry Division
www.tourism.gov.np

Riding white horses, New Zealand
Pakiri Beach Horse Riding
www.ridenz.com

Tourism New Zealand
www.newzealand.com

River-running, Zambia
Sun International
www.suninternational.com

Zambia National Tourist Board
www.zambiatourism.com

Sea-kayaking Baja, Mexico
Baja Outdoor Activities
www.kayactivities.com

Mexico Tourism Board
www.visitmexico.com

**Searching for pearls, French
Polynesia**
Tahiti Tourism Board
www.tahiti-tourisme.pf

Skiing the Vallée Blanche, France
Chamonix Tourist Office
www.chamonix.com

Neilson
www.neilson.com

Souk shopping, Morocco
Dar Les Cigognes
www.lescigognes.com

Moroccan National Tourist Office
www.tourism-in-morocco.com

**Swimming in thermal spas,
Iceland**
Iceland Tourist Board
www.icetourist.is

Tasting warrior life, Mongolia
Mongolia Tourism Board
www.mongoliatourism.gov.mn

Nomads Tours & Expeditions
www.nomadstours.com

Tracking spirit bears, Canada
BC Ferries
www.bcferries.com

Klemtu Tourism
www.klemtutourism.com

**Trekking the Milford Track,
New Zealand**
Dairy Guest House, Queenstown
www.thedairy.co.nz

Real Journeys
www.realjourneys.co.nz

Ultimate Hikes
www.ultimatehikes.co.nz

Trekking Torres del Paine, Chile
Blue Green Adventures
www.lastfrontiers.com/bluegreen

Chile Tourism Promotion
Corporation
www.visit-chile.org

Walking the Wall, China
China National Tourist Office
www.cnto.org

Watching Aida, Italy
Arena di Verona
www.arena.it

Italian Tourism
www.enit.it

Tourism Portal of the District of
Verona
www.tourism.verona.it/eng/

A FIREFLY BOOK

Published by Firefly Books Ltd. 2005

First published in 2005 by BBC Books Ltd.
BBC worldwide Ltd., Woodlands, 80 Wood Lane, London, W12 0TT

Third printing 2006

Publisher Cataloging-in-Publication Data (U.S.)

Watkins, Steve.
   Unforgettable things to do before you die / Steve Watkins and
Clare Jones.
[256] p. : col. photos. ; cm.
Summary: Guide to forty interesting and unusual activities to do in
destinations around the world.
ISBN-13: 978-1-55407-064-0 (pbk.)
ISBN-10: 1-55407-064-3 (pbk.)
1. Special events – Guidebooks. 2. Conduct of life – Miscellanea.
I. Title.
170/.44 22   BJ1585.W38   2005

National Library of Canada Cataloguing in Publication

Watkins, Steve
   Unforgettable things to do before you die / Steve Watkins and
Clare Jones.
ISBN-13: 978-1-55407-064-0
ISBN-10: 1-55407-064-3
1. Travel--Guidebooks. 2. Voyages and travels--Pictorial works.
I. Jones, Clare II. Title.
G153.4.W38 2005   10'.2'02   C2004-906966-7

Published in the United States by   Published in Canada by
Firefly Books (U.S.) Inc.   Firefly Books Ltd.
P.O. Box 1338, Ellicott Station   66 Leek Crescent
Buffalo, New York 14205   Richmond Hill, Ontario L4B 1H1

Designer: Bobby Birchall (DW Design)

Printing and color origination by Butler & Tanner Ltd., Frome,
Great Britian

**This book is dedicated to the
memory of Steve's father,
Don Watkins.
Forever smiling and a passionate
traveller, he provided endless
inspiration, encouragement
and support.**

Acknowledgements

Special thanks to Nicky Ross, Christopher
Tinker, Anthea Bull and David Cottingham
at BBC Worldwide; Bobby Birchall at DW
Design; and Tessa Clark, for their support,
professionalism and enthusiasm.

We would also like to thank the following
for their help, advice and company during
this project: Phil Nelson at Surf-Lines,
Emily Grubb, Lalla Dutt and Martin Petts at
BGB Associates, Neil Rogers, Amrit Singh,
Vivek Angra, Sinna, Paul and Anne Leeson,
Josie Heisig, Mick and Lucy Fleming,
Charles Metcalfe, Andre Schoeman, Evan
Loveless, Chris Aldilidge, Bat Bayar, Walaa
Ezz El Din, Omar Masarweh, David Symes,
Sarah Hopkins, Gillian Monahan, Gerard
Braud, Chris Ladd, Jeff Collman, Ian
Cheshire, Carter, Asma Rasheed, Elvis
Barnabas, Ben and Alejandra Gillam,
Manuel Rodriguez, Gordon Steer, Charlie
Holmes, Vietnam Tour 04, Alex Nicolson,
Peter and Heather Smith.